TH...
12 WEEK PLAN

HEALING & INSPIRING GUIDE FOR DAILY LIVING

CREATED BY

PENNY REID

EVERY STEP OF THE WAY
ONE DAY AT A TIME

Design by James Reid

The Twelve Steps

1. We admitted we were powerless over alcohol -that our lives had become unmanageable.

2. Came to believe that a Power greater than ourselves could restore us to sanity.

3. Made a decision to turn our will and our lives over to the care of God as we understood Him.

4. Made a searching and fearless moral inventory of ourselves.

5. Admitted to God, to ourselves, and to another human being the exact nature of our wrongs.

6. Were entirely ready to have God remove all these defects of character.

7. Humbly asked Him to remove our shortcomings.

8. Made a list of all persons we had harmed, and became willing to make amends to them all.

9. Made direct amends to such people wherever possible, except when to do so would injure them or others.

10. Continued to take personal inventory and when we were wrong promptly admitted it.

11. Sought through prayer and meditation to improve our conscious contact with God as we understood Him, praying only for knowledge of His will for us and the power to carry that out.

12. Having had a spiritual awakening as the result of these steps, we tried to carry this message to alcoholics, and to practice these principles in all our affairs.

Dedication

This journal is lovingly dedicated to all who seek truth and love, and who remind me on a daily basis just how precious life is.

Responibility Declaration

**When anyone anywhere reaches out for help I
want the hand of AA always to be there and
for that I am responsible.**

THANK YOU

I want to give a very special thank-you to my son, Jimmy, who has spent hours upon hours not only editing and formatting this book, but also bringing the pages of it to life. I could not have done it without his help. It was truly a labor of love, and I am forever grateful.

CONTENTS

INTRODUCTION

Because of Alcoholics Anonymous, I've begun an incredible, life-changing, life-affirming spiritual journey in sobriety. That I am here at all is truly a miracle! Since 1935 the 12 Steps of AA has become a way of life for millions of people the world over to change the course of their lives. Like so many other alcoholics, my life wasn't working, and I really didn't understand what was wrong with me for a very long time. I couldn't find any joy in my own life. I grew up terrified of the world around me. My life had been reduced to a daily survival game and a never-ending flight from reality. Instead of expending my energy on living my life, I had focused almost entirely on avoiding life's pain. Whatever relieved my discomfort and pain became my priority. All my attention went into "managing" this disease, including all the lying, the cover-ups, the secrecy and the denial, the manipulations, the rationalizations and all the fault-finding, which are all part of this disease. Alcohol had become my solution to everything, and near the end of my drinking, I couldn't imagine my life without it. Alcohol had become as important as the air I breathed. And in the end, alcohol dictated how I spent all my waking hours. I found myself in the grips of an addictive process more powerful than me.

Alcoholism is an obsession of the mind that condemns one to drink, and an allergy of the body that condemns one to die. I found myself on an ever narrowing, self-destructive path leading to insanity, jail and even death. When I withdrew from my life, I remained trapped in a world I needed to leave behind. My alcoholism had become my "jail", my solitary confinement, and it grew stronger in my denial. I knew that I had to find a way to stop the downward spiral I found myself in. I knew that until I could look at my life honestly and see how this disease was working in my own life, I would never be free of my addiction. Until I could see that I had been seeking comfort and answers in the very thing that was determined to destroy me, it would be very difficult, if not impossible, to do anything about it.

As my alcoholism progressed, I could no longer separate me from the disease – we had become one in the same! I came to believe that my disease was my identity. In my closed and sick mind, I failed to understand that alcoholism is a disease; there are no villains. All my life I thought I could do anything I set my mind to do, yet more and more I found myself unable to cope with life, drunk or sober. I had spent years wondering how an intelligent human being like me could ever have gotten into such a mess. Little did I realize back then all the devastation my drinking had in store for me! I learned that alcohol was only a symptom of a much deeper and complex problem, and it wasn't until all the painful consequences of my drinking had become truly unbearable that I became ready and willing to go to any lengths to stay sober and do the work necessary to begin recovery. From the moment I surrendered and began to accept the reality of my life, things began to change for the better. In surrender I found the seeds of victory. I knew the fight was over. I had become so tired of running from myself, my past and from life itself. It was time for the healing to begin. I was finally out of answers. I became empowered in a different way. My energies finally became channeled in ways that worked for me, not against me. Little by little, I've been able to discard my old life for a one that works under all conditions, one day at a time.

It was in the rooms of Alcoholics Anonymous where I found other people who were hurting too. Many of them had lost everything, yet they were able to turn their lives around. Here were men and women who were recovering from a seemingly hopeless state of mind and body. They shared how, by working the Steps, they were shown a way out of their pain and misery. They had found solutions to problems that I myself had been seeking for so long. They found a way to live in the real world, not escape from it. They found a way to open up instead of withdrawing deeper into oblivion. It all began with the 12 Steps of AA. I too began to put these Steps to work in my own life. There are no shortcuts or magic formulas to make this addiction go away. Alcoholism is a progressive disease that can never be cured; it can only be arrested one day at a time. We can access their healing power by working them on a daily basis. The 12 Steps become the guiding force in our lives. We work them until they become part of us.

My steadfast belief in them has prompted me to write a book about them called, "The 12 Step-12 Week Plan – A Guide For Daily Living", to help those entering recovery gain a better understanding of the Steps, enabling them to live their lives more fully, one day at a time. This book is in a 12 week format, in which each Step is studied and worked on for 7 days. In the beginning of each Step there is an overview paragraph on that Step, followed by a quotation and descriptive paragraph pertaining to it. Lastly, I pose questions calling for personal and thoughtful reflection on how the Step might be applied in one's own life. Fully integrating these Steps into our lives becomes an on-going part of our recovery. For most of us, the struggle to get to the place we are today has been long, lonely and painful. The Steps should not be rushed through. We can't do a lifetime of repairs and expect our lives to change overnight. Be content to grow a little each day. Our understanding of the Steps will change as we continue to heal, change and grow.

Alcoholics Anonymous is also a spiritual program, and The Steps help us to grow in our understanding of a power greater than ourselves. In recovery we become willing to grow along spiritual lines. The spiritual power of the 12 Steps can not be underestimated. Daily contact with a Higher Power is imperative for recovery. Spirituality is not something we practice only when we pray and meditate, but is reflected in everything we say and do. Our strength and intelligence are no match for this disease. We gradually become aware of the limits of our human capabilities. I've proven time and time again that when I tried living my life on my own terms, I failed miserably. Headstrong and full of ego and self-will run riot, my self-reliance has gotten me into more trouble than I care to remember. Our strong wills had to be redirected. Because of AA, we've been granted an extended remission and daily probation from this disease, but it is contingent upon our spiritual condition. AA is not a resting place. We either move forward spiritually or we regress back into our active addiction. There is no cure for this disease, only daily acceptance.

I may have originally come to AA to stop the pain and my incomprehensible demoralization, but because I stayed, I got a beautiful and sober life in return. Thanks to the daily discipline of the 12 Steps, my once unmanageable life has been transformed into something quite extraordinary. Recovery has restored my vision of things as they really are. I know that I am a much better person today than I could have ever been without AA. If it wasn't for the 12 Steps I might never have known that I am capable of acting responsibly on my own behalf in a time of crisis. I'm slowly rediscovering the person God created me to be. The Steps are my life today and there has been a wonderful weaving of the Steps into every area of my life. We need to return to the Steps again and again. They are something we "live" for the rest of our lives. The real joy of life is found in the daily living of it; it's all about the on-going process of self-discovery. Working the Steps can be overwhelming to many entering recovery, and I hope this book will become a source of inspiration as well as an on-going working guide and learning experience for anyone seeking lasting change from the effects of this deadly disease.

My journey in AA began with my acknowledgement of personal powerlessness, and from that moment on, my life has continued to improve. It was hard not to drink in the beginning, and many of us did go back out and drank again before we could get a foothold in sobriety. The Steps taught me how not to drink, but they also taught me how to live – one day at a time. I'm no longer at the mercy of alcohol that told me time and time again that the only answer was to drink. If you want Sobriety more than anything else and are prepared to go to any lengths, then there is nothing that can stop you. Each of us has a unique journey ahead of us. The good news is that we don't have to stay stuck in our misery and dysfunctional attempts at living any longer. AA is not something we join, it is something we live for the rest of our lives. Who of us ever thought that we would end up in AA and identify as an alcoholic after taking our first drink so many years ago? Who ever would have thought that AA would be our fate and our salvation? We've emerged from the most painful times of our lives with a stronger sense of who we really are. How could I stay mad at something that has taught me and given me so much? Each mistake, setback and failure in life has given me clarity, empathy and wisdom. It has all been a part of my journey. We become more than devoted followers in the program. We become living demonstrations , and some day it will be our turn to guide others.

Life is not a problem to be solved, but is a wonderful mystery to be embraced, lived and experienced. My life is so different today. I can't be so afraid of life. A new world has opened up to me. I'm grateful to be a part of a loving fellowship that has loved me back to life. AA has filled my days with loving and caring friends, genuine laughter, and a sense of renewed purpose. As long as we don't drink today, tomorrow will take care of itself. We don't know what the future holds. Today is all we have to work with. Today we can do something about it. Remember, you are the architect of your own destiny. I finally became aware that our lives could amount to more than a succession of painful days to be survived. I pray that everyone entering recovery experiences their own moment of clarity. Something quite amazing definitely happened to me on that fateful day, and it changed my life forever. Don't settle for less than an extraordinary life.

LAUGHTER IN SOBRIETY

IN PREPARING THIS BOOK, I WANTED TO APPROACH IT WITH A SENSE OF HUMOR,

THERE WAS A TIME WHEN LAUGHTER WAS ONE OF THE MOST PAINFUL SOUNDS I KNEW, AND WAS SORELY MISSING IN MY LIFE. ONE OF THE MOST TREASURED GIFTS THAT I'VE RECEIVED IN SO-BRIETY, AND PERHAPS THE MOST OVERLOOKED AND UNDERRATED, HAS BEEN THE GIFT OF LAUGHTER. TO MY PLEASANT SURPRISE, LAUGHTER BECAME THE MAGIC AND MISSING INGREDIENT IN MY RECOVERY. SOBRIETY IS NOT ALL DOOM AND GLOOM. IF SOBRI-ETY WASN'T FUN, NO ONE WOULD STICK AROUND! WE NEEDED TO GIVE OURSELVES PERMISSION TO LAUGH. THERE IS GREAT HEALING POWER IN LAUGH-TER, AND IF THERE EVER WAS A TIME WHEN WE NEEDED A SENSE OF HUMOR, IT WAS NOW! WHEN I WAS ABLE TO LAUGH AGAIN, ESPECIALLY AT MYSELF, I KNEW THAT I WAS BEING RESTORED TO SANITY. LAUGHTER BECAME A POSITIVE EXPRESSION OF AC-CEPTANCE, UNDERSTANDING AND FORGIVENESS ; A CONTAGIOUS AND HEALTHY RESPONSE TO LIFE, PUT-TING EVERYTHING IN IT'S PROPER PERSPECTIVE. WE WERE FINALLY ABLE TO LOOK AT OUR OWN LIVES FINDING HUMOR IN THE INSANITY OF IT ALL.

DO NOT BE DISCOURAGED. NO ONE AMONG US HAS BEEN ABLE TO MAINTAIN ANYTHING LIKE PERFECT ADHERENCE TO THESE PRINCIPLES. WE ARE NOT SAINTS. THE POINT IS, THAT WE ARE WILLING TO GROW ALONG SPIRITUAL LINES. THE PRINCIPLES WE HAVE SET DOWN ARE GUIDES TO PROGRESS. WE CLAIM SPIRITUAL PROGRESS RATHER THAN SPIRITUAL PERFECTION."

- Big Book , pg. 60

...WE AREN'T A GLUM LOT. IF NEWCOMERS COULD SEE NO JOY OR FUN IN OUR EXISTENCE, THEY WOULDN'T WANT IT. WE ABSOLUTELY INSIST ON ENJOYING LIFE.

~Big Book , pg. 132

1

STEP ONE

> WE ADMITTED WE WERE POWERLESS OVER ALCOHOL — THAT OUR LIVES HAD BECOME UNMANAGEABLE

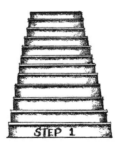

STEP 1

MY SPIRITUAL JOURNEY OF RECOVERY BEGAN WITH MY ACKNOWLEDGEMENT OF PERSONAL POWERLESSNESS. I HAD HONESTLY THOUGHT I COULD DO ANYTHING I SET MY MIND TO. BUT, BY ATTEMPTING TO EXERT CONTROL OVER EVERY ASPECT OF MY LIFE – ESPECIALLY MY ADDICTION TO ALCOHOL – MY LIFE BECAME UNMANAGEABLE. I DIDN'T HAVE THE POWER AND CONTROL I ONCE THOUGHT I HAD; I HAD ONLY LIVED WITH THE ILLUSION OF CONTROL. MY LIFE WASN'T WORKING. I HAD BEEN ON A PATH LEADING TO INSANITY AND DEATH. I WAS IN THE GRIPS OF AN ADDICTIVE PROCESS THAT HAD RENDERED ME POWERLESS OVER MY ACTIONS AND BEHAVIORS. I FELT CONFUSED, LOST, EMPTY AND SCARED. I NEEDED TO CHANGE, BUT I DIDN'T KNOW HOW TO LIVE MY LIFE ANY DIFFERENTLY. FOR MOST OF US, COMING TO AA FOR HELP WAS A LAST RESORT. I HAD NOWHERE ELSE TO GO WITH MY PAIN. I NEVER DREAMED ALCOHOL COULD BE AT THE ROOT OF MY TROUBLES. AS LONG AS I CONTINUED TO BELIEVE THAT I WAS IN CONTROL, I WOULD CONTINUE TO FIGHT A BATTLE I COULD NEVER WIN. OVER TIME THIS DISEASE GETS WORSE, NEVER BETTER. IF I DRANK AGAIN I WOULD PROBABLY DIE. I BECAME READY TO GO TO ANY LENGTH TO GET WELL. BY ACKNOWLEDGING MY ALCOHOLISM, I COULD BEGIN TO HEAL. AA HELPED ME TO MAKE SENSE OUT OF MY INSANITY. STEP ONE IS THE FIRST STEP IN OUR JOURNEY TOWARDS WHOLENESS AND AUTHENTICITY AND FORMS THE FOUNDATION FOR THE REMAINING STEPS. IN RECOVERY WE LEAVE OUR ALCOHOLIC WORLD BEHIND US. LIKE AN INFANT TAKING HIS FIRST STEPS IN LEARNING TO WALK, WE IN AA ARE TAKING OUR FIRST STEP TO A NEW AND BEAUTIFUL LIFE.

Results? Why, man I have gotten a lot of results. I know several thousand things that won't work."

–Thomas Alva Edison

One extremely important spiritual principle is the idea of accepting "what is" instead of insisting that life be a certain way. So many of our internal struggles arise from our need to control our lives. I had wasted so much precious time and energy stubbornly trying to control and solve things I couldn't. I had reached a point in my drinking career where I could no longer fight, manipulate, cheat, finagle, lie, beg, borrow or steal my way out of the mistakes I had made while under the influence. There is no more bargaining or negotiating, no more broken promises, no more pat answers or smart replies! My alcoholism had been in control, and drinking had become the biggest part of my day. I couldn't function without it. Episodic relapses had become more frequent, each one increasing my feelings of helplessness, shame and guilt. All my resistance and self-will had kept me trapped in a way of life that I longed to be free of.

WHAT I WAS EXPERIENCING, WAS HELL ON EARTH. MY LIFE HAD BECOME SO UNMANAGEABLE, THAT CHANGING MY BEHAVIOR BECAME MY ONLY OPTION, NEXT TO INSANITY OR DEATH.

I had to, once and for all, stop fighting everything and everyone. This illness was more powerful than me. I finally became ready to listen. Each of us had to reach that place where we were "all done". I was told that you "hit your bottom" when you stop digging. Hitting bottom is one of the most painful things we will have to go through as alcoholics, but we had to break through our demoralizing self-pity, our egos, (which were fighting for self-preservation), all our self-justifications, our pride, our arrogance and our denial. If we truly want to change something, the best starting point is acceptance. The pain we had created for ourselves was always the result of some form of non-acceptance. Acceptance is such an important part of our happiness, contentment and healthy growth, and is the magic word that makes this monumental change possible. The greater our acceptance and surrender to this truth, the greater our serenity will be. We've discovered that we can survive and even grow in difficult times. It empowers the positive, and allows us to begin to find out what we need to do to take healthy care of ourselves on a daily basis. Focus more on becoming peaceful where you are, instead of focusing on where you'd rather be. Let this moment be the turning point in your life. You will find a peace that you can carry with you as you go through your day.

• *What is your definition of sanity?*

" *Life begins on the other side of despair."*

–Jean–Paul Sartre

The journey of recovery begins at the end of the road; AA is the last house on the block. After so many false and shaky starts in recovery, I finally realized that I had just about used up all my options to stop drinking. I found myself on a dead end street. I had no where else to run to; I had no where else to go with my pain. Each day had become a greater struggle for me to survive. It was at this crucial cross road that I found AA. It had taken most of us a very long time to identify as an alcoholic, but we became desperate to find new solutions. Most of us had tried going it alone, secretly hoping to merely control our drinking. But, we learned the hard way that half measures simply didn't work! We can't get and remain sober by ourselves. Friends and family, as hard as they tried to understand and help, and as well-meaning as they were, couldn't begin to know the shame, the pain and the loneliness caused by this disease. Recognizing when we need help and knowing where to find it is so crucial for our survival. In AA I found others who felt like I did, who were just as frightened, insecure and unable to cope with life as I was. I heard my fears, concerns and doubts being shared by others. These meetings became my home. It is where I found myself, a shared hope, tolerance and unconditional love. It is where I can share my experiences, talk about my pain, learn from my mistakes and identify with others' pain and struggles. Meetings are where I've found a sense of belonging. It is where I've come to rely on and genuinely care about someone other than myself. Meetings are where I've learned to take responsibility for my own life, starting with taking commitments. I was told if I don't pick up the first drink, I'll always have hope. Refusing to hope is nothing more than a decision to die. Meetings keep me alive by providing a safe haven where I can continue to heal and build a new life, one glorious day at a time. It was in meetings that I've witnessed the triumph of the human spirit overcoming impossible odds to find peace and joy. Meetings are where I am loved for who I am. When I look into others' eyes, I can tell they really see the real me. Meetings are where I am told to keep coming back.

• *What events in your life caused you to realize the extent of your pain?*

• *When did you finally identify as an alcoholic?*

By going back in our own drinking histories we could show that years before we were out of control that our drinking even then was no mere habit that it was indeed the beginning of a fatal progression.

–Twelve and Twelve

Reality interfered with all my plans. I've spent years denying and insulating myself from all the unpleasantness in life. How clouded my vision became over the years! I just didn't want to face the consequences of my drinking and the impact it had on my life, resulting in a lifetime of secrecy and cover-ups. Denial became an indispensable survival device and coping behavior, protecting me from things too overwhelming and painful to see and feel. Sadly, my disease grew stronger in my denial. I became good at ignoring problems, hoping and praying they'd magically disappear on their own. Sadly, this disease can't be willed away. I rationalized problems too, telling myself that things weren't as bad as they seemed. I even blamed others for my sad state of affairs. But, I wasn't happy, joyous or free. I knew the time was coming when I wouldn't be able to hold onto my job, my marriage, my health or my dreams. I knew, deep down, that if I continued to drink, everything meaningful in my life would soon be gone. Alcohol was slowly, and ever so gradually, taking away all my choices. I no longer felt that I had the choice to stop. This disease is stronger than I am. It gave me a false sense of pleasure that invariably turned into pain. I knew without a doubt, that alcohol was killing me. Maintaining this illusion of control became hazardous to my health. I didn't have the power and control I thought I had. Alcohol ran my life, and had affected every aspect of my life. Time was running out; I've denied the whole truth long enough. I had to address my false sense of well-being. There may be a few of us who haven't lost their jobs, their homes, their friends, their families or their respectability, YET. There may be some of us who haven't been faced with financial or legal problems, YET. There may even be some who haven't become unreliable or irresponsible, YET. Some of us may not even have had DUI's, jail time, community service, or ER visits looming over us YET. But, it's only a matter of time. When I became desperate enough, I embraced the idea of acceptance –

the only real source of serenity and peace. I had to review my drinking history and face the truth about where my drinking had taken me. For years we told ourselves and others that we'd quit "someday". Someone reminded me that there are 7 days in a week, and someday isn't one of them! I once thought alcohol was the only thing that made my life bearable. There was a time when I thought my life would be over without drinking. Ironically, I feel like I've just begun to live. I'm in a much better place today. I've emerged from some of the most painful times I've ever had to deal with; coming face to face with this pain has been an important part of the healing process. We can't heal and change what we refuse to confront. Am I finally convinced I'm powerless over my disease before everything meaningful in my life is gone? Half measures availed us nothing.

• *Are you finally convinced that time has run out?*

❝ It is the true nature of mankind to learn from mistakes, not from example. ❞

-FRED HOYLE

Surrender? Me? Unthinkable! There was a time when I couldn't imagine a life without drinking in it. Drinking was the only thing that made my miserable life bearable. But, in the end, I had to take a long, hard look at my life and my alcoholism to see where my self-will had led me. I had to admit that perhaps I couldn't run the whole show by myself! It was hard for me to accept that I did not always know what was best for me. My alcoholic personality tended to be grandiose. It had allowed me to think that I was master of my own destiny, believing that self-reliance and self-sufficiency were attributes to be admired. The reality is that too many of us have died trying to preserve our independence. We had to come to grips with the reality of our lives and admit we need help. The bottom line was that I was truly powerless over alcohol, and that my best efforts to get and stay sober weren't good enough. Problems are not put in our lives to defeat us, and no problem comes to us that doesn't have a purpose in our lives. Problems come in all shapes and sizes and they all present us with something we wish were different. Rest assured, problems will be repeated until they are learned. Problems can also become an opportunity as a potential source of a greater awakening. We're here to learn from the natural consequences of our actions, and to gain the wisdom necessary to progress on our path of spiritual enlightenment and a sober life. We need to appreciate them for what they are – precious life lessons! When we make mistakes, the worst thing we can do is to pretend that we didn't make any. We should be grateful for them. We'll live and learn, rise and fall, and fail and succeed. We'll get a chance to do better the next time. We need to stop looking for the easy way. I had failed to conquer my alcoholism. It took me a long time to accept this fact. I had to surrender to win. Through surrender, a whole new and wonderful world has opened up for me, with new friends, new dreams, new priorities and new attitudes. I've come alive; I feel like I've been reborn! Every step taken from that moment of surrender, has been a step in the right direction. AA made me see how important it was for me to remember my past as it really was!

• *What frightened you most about surrendering control and admitting you needed help?*

> **The idea that somehow, some day he will control and enjoy his drinking, is the great obsession of every abnormal drinker. The persistence of this illusion is astonishing. Many pursue it to the gates of insanity or death."**

Alcoholics Anonymous

Drinking had become my great obsession and crutch. Looking back, I saw how I needed a drink before I could function and start my day. Even the simplest of errands or dealings with other people were too overwhelming for me. I spent so much time and energy trying to behave like "normal" people, but I needed a drink to do it! Part of the seduction of this disease was that it made us feel as if we could do anything and gave us a sense of belonging. By every form of self-deception and experimentation I tried to prove myself an exception to the rule. These ongoing fears and inadequacies, along with my compulsive need to manage, ultimately stood in the way of the help I needed to begin my recovery. This need for control would prove fatal to my sobriety. I rarely got the results I wanted, but what I did get was an unmanageable life. I could no longer rely on my self-will to direct my life. In many ways I had become my own worst enemy. Although it is different for each of us, there comes a moment of clarity when we can finally see that our drinking was interfering with the quality of our lives. It had been our honest belief that we had a handle on things, and that we were "managing" our own lives quite well. We were so focused on having control that we couldn't see how out of control we had become! We were in the grips of an addictive process that had rendered us powerless over our actions and behavior. After thousands of second chances, it was time to stop and take stock of where all our efforts and self-defeating behaviors had taken us. Up to now, denial acted as a shield against my facing life as it really was. Looking back, my drinking life had not been a happy one. How foolish I was to believe that drinking could still be fun!

No alcoholic ever recovers control. Over time this disease gets worse, never better. I found that there are things worse that dying. I had been experiencing a very slow, progressive, self-induced suicide. Until we reach that intolerable threshold of pain could we begin to take the first step. If I ever thought I had regained control of my drinking, I would drink again and probably die. Powerlessness is the all important key to recovery. On my own, I could do nothing to overcome the power of alcohol. Do I finally understand the fatal nature of my situation? In the beginning, I didn't want to know how sick I was, and when I was finally ready to become aware of this fact, I was amazed at all the ways I had been fooling myself! AA helped me to make sense out of my insanity. I was like a patient trying to perform surgery on himself! This attempt to fix myself only ended in greater pain. The old me needed to die.

• *When did your moment of clarity come?*

" *The strongest rebellion may be expressed in quiet, un-dramatic behavior."*

—Benjamin Spock

I lacked serenity. My search for peace of mind was an unending quest for me. Patience was a quality that frequently eluded me. Broadsided by circumstances beyond my control, I found myself helplessly propelled towards destruction as I tried coping with the demands of everyday living. With today's timetables, schedules and deadlines, peace of mind seemed less attainable than ever. As the pace of our lives accelerated, I became a slave to worry, anxiety, indecision and stress. My usual frantic behavior was not a healthy and reliable foundation for my new and sober way of life. Resistance meant struggle for me. I've spent most of my life reacting to problems rather than trying to solve them by thinking them through. My runaway mind usually raced from one crisis to another, often missing the lessons they were trying to teach me. Anxiety and dread were usually my first reaction to them, blocking much needed solutions. I became accustomed to living in chaos and confusion. How stubborn I had been towards change and doing things differently. In clearing away the wreckage of my past, I've found that there's no benefit in pushing too hard, or in being in too much of a hurry. In recovery, I'm being shown a better way to live. AA has helped me to deal with life in healthier ways and to channel my energies in a positive way, helping me to get through the awkwardness and discomfort we experience in early recovery. It's mainly a quiet battle, fought daily with willingness and patience. I'm being guided into an entirely new direction – one of faith, trust, honesty and hope. I'm finding that I have an "unsuspected inner resource", helping me to act rather than react on a daily basis. Answers can be found in the stillness within. I can pause and reflect, while asking for God's guidance. I became willing to allow God to spread His calming presence over my man-made confusion. I need to remember that we are never given more than we can handle. Gone is the drama, the urgency, the insanity and the inner turmoil that has caused me so much anguish. Serenity will be mine as a result of working the Steps. I'm still learning to let go of situations I can't control. This admission of powerlessness is the first step towards achieving this serenity. When I'm admitting powerlessness, what am I really giving up? My misery? My discomfort? As I grow in faith, I can begin to trust that all is well. Sobriety needs to be a positive experience, but it doesn't happen overnight. It's a lifelong undertaking – one day at a time. Let today happen. Give it your quiet and undivided attention. It's the peace and serenity that keeps me coming back. The world was not in disarray, I was! Life's lessons are simple once we give up the struggle. Today my life is in a state of synchronicity because of AA.

• *What kind of frantic behaviors did you resort to when faced with unexpected problems?*

• *How do you handle stress today?*

" *It is the individual who knows how little he knows about himself who stands a reasonable chance of finding out something about himself."*

- S.I. HAYAKAWA

I have a tendency to live inside my head, yet I'm finding out more and more that knowledge isn't all it's cracked up to be. We don't always know what is best for us. Our alcoholic personality tended to be grandiose, egocentric and self-centered. In AA we learn that we don't know everything. We're not all-knowing and all-powerful. There are limits to what we can do by ourselves. We needed to exchange our pride with a dose of humility. One of the most important things we learn to do in the program is recognize when something isn't working. We were told that our best thinking got us here. Alcoholism is not only a drinking disease, it is also a thinking disease. We had thought that our minds and intelligence were running the show. Yet our minds remained cluttered with out-of-date data and ready made answers and misperceptions. We were the victim of our own faulty thinking. We've spent years analyzing this disease, trying to find the causes and cures. We rationalized and excused our behaviors beyond all reason. We convinced ourselves we knew why we drank, yet we became alcoholics anyway! Too many of us have died looking for these reasons. I drank because I have the disease of alcoholism; I don't need any other reason. In recovery we begin to take an objective look at ourselves and our misguided thinking. We had no choice but to become more open-minded. We needed to be reprogrammed. We had a great deal to learn and unlearn about this disease, but this could only happen if we remain teachable. It all comes down to ego deflation. The time had come for reevaluation. We began to sort the truths and half-truths from the lies. Do we believe a reassuring lie or an inconvenient truth? Do we want to experience peace and honesty or illusion and conflict? If answers aren't readily available, we can trust that clarity will reveal itself when the time is right. I do my part and trust that God will take care of the rest. Recovery is an exciting opportunity for personal growth. We are growing and changing because of this program. I don't need all the answers today. Analyzing this disease was my attempt to control it. But we can't outsmart this disease. I honestly thought I could think my way into right action. The hard truth was that I can only act my way into right thinking. It's almost as if you have to lose yourself or be taken apart and put back together again in order to find yourself. God opened my eyes to see myself. A whole new life has opened up because I wanted something better for myself. New ideas are beginning to make sense.

•*What reasons did you think caused you to drink?*

•*With this knowledge, were you able to stay abstinent?*

2

STEP TWO

CAME TO BELIEVE
THAT A POWER GREATER
THAN OURSELVES COULD
RESTORE US TO SANITY

We begin Step Two in a state of powerlessness. All we need to begin is a belief that a power greater than ourselves is waiting to help us. Before entering recovery, we thought we needed to drink more to preserve our sanity. We believed that there was nothing another drink couldn't fix; we were so full of ourselves. Our vision had been so limited. Alcoholism is a form of insanity rendering us incapable of rational thinking and behavior. We needed to take a leap of faith. We began to seek out something greater than ourselves as a new source of help, comfort, strength and guidance. Even the smallest seed of faith was all that was needed to begin this new life. We opened our hearts and minds to the possibility that such a power could work for us as well. Today, I'm convinced that a power greater than myself picked me up off the floor and guided me to the rooms of Alcoholics Anonymous. There was something transforming that happens to us in meetings. We can't put our finger on it, but we come away with a greater sense of peace than we had when we walked in. It was the changes we saw in people that gave us the faith and hope to believe that it could work for us, too. Today, we go to meetings, reach out, share, listen and tap into an endless supply of wisdom. Miracles of recovery are evident everywhere. AA is a program in which we find spiritual solutions to the things we are powerless over. The bottom line is that we're not God. Once we accept this fact, we can begin to change. Step Two is all about hope for a saner life.

❝ I was captain of my own ship. The only trouble was my ship was completely disabled and rudderless.”

- THE GRAPEVINE

We've made a mess of trying to run our own lives. Before finding our way to AA, we resisted most everything the program stood for. We thought we knew what was best for us, and we stubbornly held on to the belief that we had all the answers. It was all about control. We were blind to the fact that we had caused so much trouble and unhappiness trying to manage everything ourselves. We began

Step Two in a state of powerlessness, finally realizing that we are powerless over much in our lives. The good news is that we don't have to control everything for our lives to work out. More and more, we are making faith and trust an ongoing part of our day-to-day living. All we needed to begin was a belief that a power greater than ourselves was waiting to help and guide us when we became ready and willing. I had no power to help myself and change the course my life had taken.

Letting go of control does not mean giving up

It does mean opening ourselves up to new ideas. When we ran the show, we were blocking God from our lives. We needed to step aside. Turning my life over to the care of a Higher Power has been the most transforming experience of my life. Life's journey can be rough and challenging, but today I have faith that I will be steered in the right direction and navigated into peaceful waters. Without a Higher Power, I was like a "storm-tossed ship without a rudder." A new world has opened up to me. My individual strength and knowledge were not enough for smooth sailing. I need my Higher Power at the helm. I gave God his job back! I have faith in something which remains a mystery to me, but I continue to seek it on a daily basis. Today, I've found the courage to face each day, knowing God is holding my world together. I needed to stay out of results and let go of the outcomes. Peace of mind is knowing that in bad times, all is good. It's letting go of yesterday and letting tomorrow take care of itself. Faith has replaced fear and uncertainty. Today I have a program that offers me the world. I will bring joy and a sense of wonder wherever I go. Let your spirit be your guide.

• *What were some of the things you had to give up control over?*

• *Has your life improved?*

66 *A wise man changes his mind,
a fool never will."*

17TH CENTURY PROVERB

D o not disturb! Alcoholics can be so stubborn! Once we get an idea in our heads, we didn't want to listen to anything new. Oh how we fought change! In the past, the first order of business had always been self-preservation. Our minds were made up; our minds were welded shut. We were convinced that our superior intelligence backed by our willpower would guarantee sobriety. It was our fear of the unknown that prevented us from moving forward with our lives. Working overtime, our frightened egos refused to learn anything new, coming up with clever rationalizations to protect us from the humiliation of being wrong. Looking back, I see that I didn't have the open-mindedness to really hear what I needed to hear to recover and heal. By the time I reached AA, my mind was open just enough to know that I needed help. (a real and honest acceptance about this disease will take more time.) Today, I am learning that when I stubbornly close the door on my mind, I am locking out far more than I'm locking in. Recovery involves a willingness to make mistakes and learn from them. My mind had remained cluttered with ready-made and out-dated answers and misperceptions. In sobriety, we give up trying to always be right and accept the fact that "we know only a little". It takes courage to take an honest look at one's life and discover what was no longer working and change it. When I could recognize my own irresponsible, weak, immature, dishonest, greedy, manipulative, pretentious, hypercritical, and lazy self, I began to respect and listen to another point-of-view. In seeking first to understand, I am putting my respect for another person above my need to be right. Is expanding our mind and opening up our heart to new ideas such a bad thing? Is our way the only way to look at something? Because of our ego's pride and stubbornness, we lost out on some wonderful ways to improve and enrich our lives. A whole new life has opened up because I wanted something better for myself. Let go of the ego. Start asking questions! Once a mind is stretched, it can never go back to its original dimension. New ideas are beginning to make sense. We are growing and changing as a result of our commitment to this incredible program. Having a closed mind is unfortunate because there is so much we can learn from points of view different from our own. A closed mind is a dangerous thing.

• *What new ideas are you opening up to?*

" *An unshared life is not living. He who shares does not lessen, but greatens his life."*

–STEPHEN S. WISE

Alcoholism is a disease that thrives on progressive isolation. We suffered in agonizing silence, feeling dan-
gerously vulnerable. Our lives were becoming increasingly unmanageable; each day became more of a struggle for
us. Many of us shut down completely and became unavailable. We had become experts at keeping secrets and avoiding
others. We hid our insecurities at all costs. To recover we
needed to reach out and risk exposing our vulnerable human
side with all our hurts and fears. We needed to be able to talk
about the things that were troubling us. Much of recovery
involves learning how to share and express our feelings and
fears in healthy ways with others in recovery. Part of our isolation grew out of a belief that we were unique, believing that
no one had done or said or felt the terrible things that we did.
At first we thought sharing would only add to our pain and
discomfort, but we soon found that this honest sharing is
what makes the difference between living and dying for those
of us who seek shelter in AA. Sharing allowed us to see how
much alike we are. I began to see myself in others. I began
to believe that someone else on the planet knew how I felt!
We heard our stories being told. When we share, we break
through our isolation and begin to find solutions and answers
to problems that had once seemed impossible to deal with
when they remained trapped inside our heads. Recovery is a
shared experience and a shared hope. Sharing is how we heal.
Sharing becomes a way of life for us. Finding the willingness
to admit we need help can be one of the hardest challenges

for us in early recovery. It's so important to let others be there for us. Reaching out is the key to recovery. Here I found real friends who shared difficult truths that they didn't want to face or deal with. Here I observed the strength and courage they exhibited in getting and staying sober. It was in the rooms of AA that love began to infiltrate our lives.

WHEN WE LIVE IN LOVE, IT CHANGES OUR PERCEPTION OF EVERYTHING.

For many of us it was the first time we had experienced love in a non-judgmental, non-manipulative, honest and selfless way. Our hearts opened and we let the world in. Sharing is how we are set free. We are sober, our minds are clear, we have new hope and we've regained trust.

- *What secrets were you afraid to share with others thinking no one would understand?*

- *When you did share them, how did it make you feel?*

" Maturity begins to grow when you can sense your concern for others outweighingyour concern for yourself"

–John MacNaughton

I need to go to meetings. Where else but in A.A. could you find millions of people dedicated to love, and being there for one another? Up to now, it was all about me; I was self-willed, self-seeking and self-centered. I was too busy focusing on MY life and MY problems, to see anyone else's needs. When I got to A.A., everything changed. I was no longer the center of my universe. There's something transforming that happens to us in meetings. We begin to put ourselves in another's shoes; we begin to focus on someone else with genuine concern and compassion. It comes down to one alcoholic sharing, talking, risking and caring with another. In AA we come together for mutual survival. We see newcomers hanging around on the fringes of AA, struggling alone and confused with no recovery tools. Helping others is how we hold on to our sobriety; it's how we carry its message. The humility we acquire in sobriety is not thinking less of ourselves, but thinking more of others. Our self-esteem grows as we set up chairs, make coffee or help with clean-up. Recovery is found in the doing. Compassion becomes a verb. We cease being takers and begin being givers. Meetings are where we become right-sized and useful. We get to see the miracle of that first flicker of hope in the eyes of someone who felt hopeless. Being there for others becomes the high point of our day.

WE GO TO AA TO GET SOBER, BUT IF WE STAY LONG ENOUGH, WE LEARN A WHOLE NEW WAY OF LIVING, FILLED WITH LOVE AND SERVICE.

What a wonderful gift to leave someone feeling a little better about themselves. We let them know they count. By getting outside ourselves by helping others, we are helping ourselves. It was so easy to get trapped inside our own pain, but today we don't have to stay stuck in our misery. I felt like a sponge soaking up this new and positive way of living! I needed to take the action, and what's more, I always feel so much better after a meeting. Because of AA, I will never go back to self-centered living. We become what we do. We bring the light of hope to others still suffering. Your life becomes your message and it will inspire others. We are finally able to see that our lives do have a purpose! I am forever humbled by the wonder of it all! Without this selfless Love the heartbeat of AA would cease to beat.

MAKE A DIFFERENCE IN SOMEONE ELSE'S LIFE TODAY !

• *Have you extended*
         your hand to a
                  newcomer lately?

" *It is no good hearing an inner voice or getting an inner prompting if you do not immediately act on that inner prompting."*

–DAVID SPANGLER

How many times have we heard, "Don't drink and go to meetings!"? It's such a simple concept for us complicated alcoholics. There was nothing simple about my life before I found my way to AA. We're confronted with so many decisions in our day-to day living, yet for most of our lives, we've felt so ill-equipped to make sound decisions. My life had become too overwhelming, confusing and unmanageable. I found that there was no magic formula to achieve sobriety. The best advice I got was, "Keep it simple". One of the first things we did was to turn our lives over to a power greater than ourselves. But, we still had to do our part. Today, I have a chance to make a positive contribution to my own recovery and sense of well-being. My new sober life is built upon layers of small, manageable steps taken everyday.

RECOVERY WILL TAKE TIME, PERSEVERANCE, PATIENCE, DISCIPLINE AND ACTION.

We don't have to tackle our problems all at once, but today I know that when I'm anxious, angry, uneasy, too tired, too busy, too complacent, confused or scared, I need to get myself to a meeting. And the times I don't feel like going to a meeting is when I really need to go to one! I must never just sit and do nothing. Not taking action had become an automatic response for many of us. More and more, I realize that certain inactions can lead to a slip or worse. It doesn't matter what I believe; it's what I DO that counts. Don't wait until you have enough energy to move forward. If you start moving, the energy will be there. Get up and do something! To become accountable, we must be willing to take corrective action. We simply begin

by putting one foot in front of the other and do the next indi-
cated step. Sometimes the smallest step in the right direction
ends up being the biggest step of your life. Tip toe if you must,
but please TAKE the step! We can't stay sober on yesterday's
actions. Repeated practice is a critical part of recovery.

AA WORKS FOR THOSE WHO WORK IT!

• *Are you cultivating habits that are helpful in attaining
  your goals?*

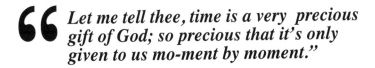

Let me tell thee, time is a very precious gift of God; so precious that it's only given to us mo-ment by moment."

–AMELIA BARR

L ife truly is a precious gift that we are given moment by moment in sobriety, and there is so much joy and happiness to be found in each and every one of these moments, but we have to know where to look. Man has been on a quest, searching everywhere for happiness - that place of joy where we are free to love and be ourselves; a place where we don't have to justify our existence or earn our happiness. It wasn't that long ago that I thought the happy times would never come again. I had looked everywhere for happiness in all the wrong places - in other people, in material things and in mood-altering chemicals. I was living in a fear-filled world. Worrying, manipulating and anticipating the worst, I had removed myself from the beauty, serenity and wonder of the present moment. Today my life has come full circle. I'm seeing as I grow in sobriety, that real happiness comes from knowing who I am, and becoming comfortable in my own skin. Today I'm open to receiving and recognizing and appreciating all the goodness, beauty, happiness and joy in my life. Life is found in the present. We need to give today our undivided attention. We need to let today happen, learn today's lessons, solve today's problems and enjoy today's gifts. Today, I'm enjoying a new and sober life, and I want to make the most of every precious minute that we are given. I see my world so differently today. With my new found sobriety, I get to experience the warmth of the sun on my face, the gentle breezes blowing through my hair, the aroma of freshly baked bread, the coolness of a refreshing mountain stream, newly fallen snow on my eyelashes, the brilliant colors of autumn leaves and glorious sunsets that will take your breath away! When I embrace this new life I've been given, I feel a deep and abiding connection with it. Let's make the most of today; we deserve to experience every bit of joy and happiness that life has to offer! I never want to take a single breath for granted. The world is an amazing place, and with each passing sober day, I am becoming more and more aware of what is right and so precious in my life. Never let another day go by without taking full advantage of all its gifts. Enjoy your journey through life with your eyes, mind and heart open to all of life's experiences. Invest your life in this moment.

• *Where do you find your happiness today?*

" To me, faith means

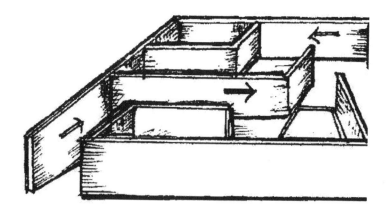

... not worrying"

– JOHN DEWEY

Looking back over my life, I had to ask myself why I didn't enjoy living more. Could it be that I was too busy borrowing tomorrow's fears and worries? Worrying had become a way of life with me, but I didn't know how to live my life any other way. Worry will never put us in a better frame of mind. I became so focused on what I didn't want, that it became all I could think about! And nothing robs us of happiness more than worry. Problems are not solved by worrying. Back then, paralyzing fears dictated all my choices. Worry won't stop the bad things from happening, it just stops us from enjoying the good things in life. I had been creating my own negative reality by continually imagining all the things that could go wrong. I was always waiting for the other shoe to drop. I had to stop obsessing about the past and future. This obsessive worrying over problems that may or may not happen is a disease of the human spirit, and implies that we don't have enough faith in a power greater than ourselves to see us through any difficulty. All my life I've wished for a life of no problems. But there does come a day when we have to come to terms with life as it is, and not how we wish it could be. I'm learning in AA that there is a wonderful purpose to problems. Without problems to grow on, there would be no opportunity for self-improvement. Problems should be guide lines, not stop signs! Perhaps the hardest part of being human is accepting our limitations and placing our trust in a Higher Power. Our need for control had prevented us from experiencing faith. But how much can God do for us if we are not open to receive His help that is available to us? Without faith in this power, chances are we won't step aside. Today I pray for knowledge of His will for me and for the inner strength to carry it out. Today my sobriety grows stronger as I learn to trust more. Trusting becomes a more positive approach to life. I'm a functioning human being again. Today we've begun to lose the fear of making decisions, and if our choice proves wrong, we can at least learn a lesson from the experience. And we don't have to figure everything out.

Our lives do have purpose and direction, and we are being guided every step of the way, one day at a time. I no longer look at problems as something to be avoided at all costs – the greater the difficulty, the greater opportunity for growth. Today I believe that there is a guiding presence in my life. We are a small part of something vast and unknown that I want to be a part of. I've grown in awareness of God's saving grace and how incredibly blessed I am. I have no illusion of what or who got me to AA. Allow God to illuminate your path. Our future is bright with promise. A sober life is full of choices. Make some smart ones!

• *When you feel lost or confused today, what actions do you take to feel safe again?*

3

STEP THREE

Made a decision to turn
our will and our lives
over to the care of God
as we understood him

STEP 3

WE ARE NO LONGER IN CHARGE. IT WAS PURE IN-SANITY TO THINK WE COULD MANAGE OUR ALREADY DYSFUNCTIONAL LIVES, LET ALONE OUR RECOVERY! IF WE ARE NOT 100% CONVINCED THAT WE ARE POWERLESS OVER ALCOHOL, AND THAT OUR LIVES ARE UNMANAGEABLE, THEN WE ARE NOT READY FOR STEP THREE. WE CAN'T BE JUST A "LITTLE" ALCOHOLIC. WE CAN'T BARTER OUR LIVES WITH GOD. IT WAS ONLY WHEN WE SURRENDERED AND LET GO OF CONTROL OVER EVERY ASPECT OF OUR LIVES, COULD OUR JOURNEY OF SOBRIETY BEGIN. OUR SOBRIETY IS NOT NE-GOTIABLE. WHATEVER WE PLACE AHEAD OF OUR SOBRIETY, THERE'S A GOOD CHANCE WE WILL LOSE IT. ONCE AND FOR ALL OUR SELF-WILL AND SELF-RELIANCE, THAT HAVE LET US DOWN AGAIN AND AGAIN, ARE NO LONGER AN OPTION FOR US IN ACHIEVING AND MAINTAINING SOBRIETY. FAITH ALONE WAS NOT ENOUGH; WE HAD TO TAKE THE ACTION TO CUT AWAY AT OUR SELF-WILL. STEP THREE IS OUR OPPORTUNITY TO START OVER. WITH THE HELP OF A HIGHER POWER'S HEALING LOVE, WE ARE FREED FROM FEELING RESPONSIBLE FOR EVERYTHING AND EVERYONE. IN THE BEGINNING WE MAY HAVE ONLY SUR-RENDERED THE "BIG" PROBLEMS. BUT, AS OUR RECOVERY PROGRESSED, SO DID OUR TRUST, UNTIL WE BECAME WILLING TO TURN OUR ENTIRE LIVES OVER TO THE CARE, LOVE AND GUIDANCE OF THIS HIGHER POWER. THE STEPS TALK ABOUT A "POWER GREATER THAN OURSELVES" AND A "GOD OF OUR OWN UNDERSTANDING". ONE OF THE MOST REMARKABLE THINGS ABOUT AA IS THAT IT ALLOWS EACH OF US TO DEFINE OUR OWN CONCEPT OF A HIGHER POWER. WE'VE BEGUN TO TURN OUR LIVES AND OUR WILLS OVER TO A POWER THAT FILLS US WITH LOVE AND ACCEPTANCE ON A DAILY BASIS. WHEN WE BECOME WILLING TO DO THIS, GOD WILL, IN RETURN, GIVE US A NEW LIFE BEYOND OUR WILDEST DREAMS. THE EMPTY HOLE INSIDE US, WHERE LONELINESS AND PAIN RESIDED, IS NOW FILLED WITH LOVE AND HOPE. AS WE BEGIN TO BUILD A NEW LIFE, WE KNOW WE WILL NEVER BE THE SAME AGAIN. WE ARE IN MUCH MORE CAPABLE HANDS TODAY.

We are the wire, God is the current. Our only power is to let the current pass through us."

–CARLO CARRETTO

Sobriety involves dealing with life on life's terms, but sobriety also involves the discovery of a Higher Power in our lives. My Higher Power is the power I plug into on a daily basis, and when I do, I am rewarded with a feeling of serenity and well-being that no amount of alcohol could ever duplicate. There are times when I still struggle to know what is my will, and what is God's will; doubt is unavoidable during times of spiritual seeking. There were so many times when I wished I had more faith. Because of Alcoholics Anonymous, my spirit becomes my inner guide. When faced with painful and difficult situations, I can plug into a loving, healing and reassuring spirit that is always with me. The more I turn over my will and life to this untapped source of strength and understanding, the more peace and serenity I find. This is a faith that works under all conditions. Instead of living in fear, constantly on the lookout for danger, and avoiding taking risks, I can now occupy myself with living and participating fully in my own life! God wants nothing more than for us to experience wonder and to spread joy. Life is a gift. But, when I lose this conscious contact, this power is shut off. When I'm unplugged from this life source, I tend to withdraw back into myself, and resort to my old ways. I can't afford to let up on this spiritual program. I need to go to meetings to remind myself how vulnerable I am when I'm "unplugged". When my ego and my fears join forces, my God-reliance goes out the window, and my insanity returns. Today, I let my Higher Power be my guide in decisions large and small. My sobriety is an on-going miracle. It's not necessary to understand everything; I just have to flip the switch, and watch sober hours turn into sober years. When I tried to solve my problems on my own, I became spiritually disconnected and I failed. But, when I'm spiritually connected, I win. By working Step Three, I've come to realize that a Power greater than myself could save me from myself. No matter how willfully I've behaved in the past, my Higher Power has never failed to pick me up and dust me off. I commit to Step Three every morning. I've become aware of an inner light deep within my very soul that the passing years will never diminish.

• *How has turning your will and life over to a Higher Power simplified your life?*

• *Are you more serene today?*

❝Change your thoughts and you change your world"

-NORMAN VINCENT PEALE

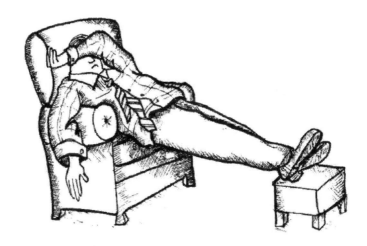

My attitude towards life has a profound affect upon what happens to me today. After years of uncontrolled drinking, I basically saw my life as a tragedy, and I was its victim, suffering daily bouts of depression, doom and gloom. I saw everything in negative terms. My daily thoughts were, "I just can't win", "nothing good ever lasts", and "it's hopeless, so why try?" Our negativity had become so embedded in our subconscious mind that it became our truth, our reality. It finally dawned on me that if I was ever going to recover from the damaging effects of this disease, I was going to have to change the way I looked at just about everything in my life! My progress in recovery depends, to a large part, on my attitude. We can manifest health, wealth and happiness as easily as illness, poverty and despair. So why do so many of us choose the negative? I've talked myself into fatigue, defeat and failure more times than I care to remember! Depression feeds on itself and becomes incapacitating, and with attention, it only gets worse. There must be something else at work. When we don't feel that we are deserving of the good things in life, it will undermine all our positive thoughts. The world had obliged my lower expectations and delivered exactly what I ordered! The more negative I became, the less my life worked. Our minds needed to be reprogrammed. As we grow spiritually, our attitudes undergo a drastic revision. In the past I always imagined the worst case scenario. I was so busy worrying and bracing myself for disappointment, that I missed out on all the joy that exists in life. What is important is this moment, and what I am choosing to think and believe right here, right now. The thoughts I project today will create my future. If I perceive myself as a failure and as a helpless victim, then I will never be able to change. Being human, we are here to transcend our limitations. The fact that we made it to the rooms of AA means that we're willing to make positive changes in our lives. Focusing on the positive is energizing. Opportunities are actually beginning to materialize where before we had only seen problems. Despair and worry had become a negative contribution to our future. When our attitude is positive, a whole new set of realities emerge. We become empowered by a very different self-perception. When we change the way we look at things, the things we look at change! I began to feel something I had not felt in years – hope. Sobriety is all about creating a good life for ourselves, offering us a new lease on life. We need to stop denying ourselves good feelings. When we create peace and harmony in our minds, we will attract it into our lives. AA has instilled in me an optimism and state of mind that refuses to let life's ups and downs hold me down any longer. Look for the positive in everything you see and do. You can begin today.

- *WHAT CHANGES IN ATTITUDE HAVE YOU NOTICED IN YOURSELF?*

- *HAVE OTHERS NOTICED CHANGES IN YOU?*

" *If you do not find peace in yourself, you will never find it anywhere else."*

-PAULA A. BENDRY

We all need quiet times to restore us to sanity. It's one of life's little joys. By putting aside our worries, even for a few moments, we are better able to put everything in its proper perspective. We've allowed ourselves to receive so little in life. Before I came to Alcoholics Anonymous, my search for inner peace was an unending quest. All I knew was how to live in a constant state of crisis in a world filled with anxiety and tension. The soft voice of my Higher Power had been silenced by the incessant chatter from the debate team inside my head. I didn't know how to feel "safe" unless I was busy. We got so use to doing something every second of the day, that it was a struggle to relax. Accepting my powerlessness and everything in my life as it is today, is the first step I needed to take to find peace of mind. We will never find peace and fulfillment until we discover it within ourselves. When we do find it, our lives will change forever. Today, I know I'm responsible for changing the things I can, and letting go of the rest. This day is too precious to waste with senseless worry. When I'm willing to work the Steps on a daily basis, I am rewarded with an inner peace that no amount of alcohol could ever have provided me with. But when I'm not willing, I'm usually restless, irritable and discontented. In sobriety, it has taken me a while to become comfortable with the stillness, but I love myself enough today by giving up all my obsessive worries. A quiet mind is the foundation for inner peace. Quiet times are vital for balancing all the external noises and confusion that infiltrates our daily lives. Just like our bodies need an occasional break from our hectic routines, our busy overactive minds need quiet times to help us balance all the confusion and noise that infiltrates much of our day. Perhaps the most important thing I can do for my sobriety and well-being today is to simply breathe deeply, go with the flow of life, live with love in my heart, be gentle and kind to myself and others, and to listen to the inner, soothing voice of my Higher Power. His spirit, strength, guidance and wisdom are as close as my breathing in and out. AA is a gentle journey of prayer and example. It is here where we get our first glimpse of what a life of inner peace is really like. It's a feeling of oneness with all creation. Nothing seems difficult. There is a calmness, serenity and an unhurriedness that is positively intoxicating, that I have never felt before. I had to stop focusing on how stressed I was and begin to think about how blessed I am.

- *WHAT THINGS CAUSED STRESS IN YOUR LIFE?*

- *WHAT DO YOU DO TODAY TO QUIET THE VOICES INSIDE YOUR HEAD?*

" *There is a divine plan of good at work in my life. I will let go and let it un-fold."*

-RUTH FREEMAN

We've come a long way in recovery, and it all started with our surrendering and turning our lives over to a Higher Power. Learning to trust is a key element in recovery. We use to worry about everything. It was hard for us to believe that everything was going to be okay. I never really considered God to be a major force in my life until I found Alcoholics Anonymous. I've even begun to pray as a direct result of working the program. Because of this action and commitment, I've been given amazing strength and faith to go on – one day at a time. My life runs so much smoother when I leave the outcome where it belongs. Letting go and trusting has become a new way of life. I've made my Higher Power my constant companion. I am never alone. He's always within my reach. His love and support surround me on a daily basis, helping me stay on course. He has become my source of confidence and strength, enabling me to face life in a new and wonderful way. With faith, my whole world seems right and on course, knowing God is holding it all together. Accept the path before you. My Higher Power has given me such a gift by allowing me to walk by faith rather than by sight. Divine order rules, and I can even let the future take care of itself. I try to take my life one day at a time. I trust God will take care of me. I know everything will workout. I know he takes care of me because I'm witnessing little miracles happening all around me, and I am one of them. A glorious world has opened up to me. As I recognize my own limitations, I'm filled with such gratitude for all the blessings I've received. I can actually feel the sunlight of his spirit. I began to feel at home in the world where everything began to look brighter, people seemed nicer and words took on deeper meaning. No one can predict what the future holds or even what's around the next corner. We don't need to know the outcome in order to keep doing the next right thing. All we can do is to make the most of each day and be reassured that our Higher Power has everything in our lives under control. I finally realized that the world is in good hands. The sun will continue to rise in the East and set in the West without any help from me. Today I am able to cope with problems that I simply couldn't have managed on my own before. What a glorious release from my self-will run riot days! Let faith be in control of every decision you make and every action you take.

• *How is your Higher Power working in your life today?*

• *Were there any experiences in your life that have made it difficult for you to trust?*

" God loves the World through US "

-MOTHER TERESA

When we arrived in AA as newcomers, we were full of anger, guilt and self-loathing. We were coming out of the darkest period of our lives. We either hated God or we gave little or no thought of Him whatsoever. Years of negative conditioning had taught us to accept, without question, every negative word, every disempowering thought and every pain that has been inflicted on us. We felt all alone as we searched and struggled daily for an identity, purpose and self-worth. If anyone needed unconditional love, we did! Recovery is an act of Love. Love opens the channel to God. We were told That God's ever present love was ours at every moment and that we are all connected through this love. All God asks of any of us is to be there for one another.

GOD USES OUR ARMS TO HOLD THOSE WHO ARE STILL SUFFERING, OUR EYES TO HELP SEE THEIR PAIN, OUR EARS TO HEAR THEIR CRIES AND OUR HEARTS TO LOVE THEM UNCONDITIONALLY.

No one wants to be forgotten, go unnoticed, feel unimportant or be taken for granted. We all want to be appreciated, touched, acknowledged, desired and respected. We all need to know that we count and that what we say does matter. This love connects us all, and is the balm that can heal our soul-sickness that we've been experiencing for so long. This love is not about approval or worthiness. It is a state of being that is forgiving, nurturing and supportive. The hugs, honest compassion and outpouring of love that I've found in the rooms of AA have changed my life forever. There can be no spirituality without loving kindness. Never underestimate the power of His love; it's transforming! Today, the desire and strength needed to grow and heal comes from loving and being loved. Today I'm free to experience a living, loving God every moment of my life. Whatever the problem – love is the answer. I don't know anyone who doesn't want a life filled with love. We need to follow where this love takes us. We begin to feel this love flow through us and out to others. If we are not giving and receiving love, we are not all that we can be. The heart is God's calling card. To know God is to be filled with a joy that goes forth to bless the entire world. It's been a curse and a blessing to feel everything so deeply. Our souls were restless until they found rest in God. Love is what we do best. Visualize God's healing light each day and send it to someone who may be hurting and in need of love. Invite God in.

- *How has God shown his love for you through others?*

• *Through a smile?*

Kind word?

Give examples...

❝ *As your faith is strengthened you will find that there is no longer the need to have a sense of control, that things will flow as they willand that you will flow with them, to your great delight and benefit"*

– EMMANUEL

Alcoholics Anonymous is a program of recovery that is spiritual in nature, and helps us grow in our understanding of God, of a power greater than ourselves. Relying on a God was foreign to many of us. I was told to surrender ALL my problems to His care and leave them there. I've learned so many of life's lessons the hard way. Again and again, I had tried controlling situations and forcing outcomes that I desired. I've been forcing square pegs into round holes for years. We've all had those not-so-together moments, whether we have one month or 30 years of sobriety. Each day life gives us more challenges. We all deserve easier lives, so it only makes sense to try learning these lessons another way. I needed a new strength beyond myself to help me face life. Instead of relying on my ego and self-will to direct my life, it was suggested that I draw upon the strength, wisdom and compassion of a Higher Power to guide me through any difficulty. Sobriety involves a series of surrenders. Life will always be a process of letting go of things beyond our control. Letting go and trusting becomes a way of life for us that will transform our lives. We've tried controlling the uncontrollable for years and where did it get us? I no longer allow the cares and worries of my day to distort my thinking. I'm no longer exhausted before my day begins by trying to micro-manage every little thing. As long as I have faith in a Higher Power and stay out of the outcomes, my path is clear. My sobriety grows stronger as I learn to trust more. If I'm willing to take the time and make the effort, my Higher Power will put me in harmony with the universe. It's such a relief to let go of all the stress and manipulation. Out of our most humiliating experiences came those moments of clarity which, in hindsight, have turned into the most beautiful blessings! My need for control prevented me from experiencing faith. It was a difficult lesson for me to learn that all my experiences are meant for my own good. Everything that happens to me has a lesson attached to it. When I allow God to show me the way, things seem to work out. But when I try to run the show or take back my problems, everything goes to Hell! The great paradox is that the less we try to manage our lives, the more effective we become at living our lives!

- *Are you calmer and more trusting and accepting of things around you today?*

❝❝ **Many people are living in an emotional jail Without realizing it."**

– VIRGINIA SATIR

My disease was my jail. I wasn't free. When I drank, I was living in a spiritual, emotional as well as physical confinement. My self-will and all my other forms of "self" had held me captive for years. Alcohol was not only an allergy of the body, but was very much an obsession of the mind. Everything in my life revolved around alcohol. I was totally preoccupied with drinking. I isolated when I drank and was very much alone. My drinking became my prison, my solitary confinement and my "singleness of purpose". All I wanted was to be left alone to drink in peace. Over the years, my drinking took on a life all its own, dictating how I live my life and the way I scheduled all my waking hours. What ever relieved my pain and discomfort became a priority in my life. This disease took away all my choices, and in the end, it came close to robbing me of life itself. I was destined to serve out a life sentence in the prison of my mind. There were days when I didn't think anyone could hurt as much as I did. Now that I'm working my program, I'm practicing a daily willingness to turn my will and my life over to a Higher Power as a kind of extended daily probation. The real answers to life's pain lies in having a strong spiritual center. For so many years God has been absent in my life. I felt empty, and nothing I tried seemed to fill the hole in my soul. Today, because of the Steps, I have found the value of life and I have discovered a God of my understanding. The Steps have helped me breakout of the prison of my old fear-based beliefs, false pride, denial and distorted misperceptions. Addiction was about separation and isolation. But there is a spirit within us that longs to be free. It was time to release any limiting, negative and self-defeating beliefs. There is a radiant, confident person hidden beneath layers of dysfunctional behaviors waiting to emerge. Recovery is all about finding the integrity and freedom to become the person we've always wanted to be. When I drank, I wanted freedom without responsibility. In sobriety these new freedoms come with great responsibility. Step Three helps us look at the world differently. There is no such thing as a pain free existence, but today I realize that life is so much more than pain, anguish, dysfunction and worry. We are finally free from the bondage of alcohol. Whoever we had been before doesn't have to limit us anymore. God doesn't take something away without putting something better in its place. In recovery we see life in a whole new light. Life is too precious to waste.

- *In what ways did alcohol become your prison?*

4

STEP FOUR

MADE A SEARCHING AND FEARLESS
MORAL INVENTORY OF OURSELVES

In recovery, our journey to wholeness would be incomplete without doing an inventory. Many of us wanted to avoid doing the 4th step. We kept putting it off, but this step of serious self-searching lays the crucial foundation for our new and sober lives. There were areas in our lives that needed our attention. We needed to understand what had been causing our soul sickness. We had to find the willingness to put pen to paper. We needed to see the parts of us we've hidden away and repressed, that were preventing us from loving ourselves and others, and keeping us from becoming the person we wanted to become. It was important to understand how our addiction acts, thinks, and feels. We began to recognize the role denial has played in our lives. We've ignored the real problems with elaborate explanations and clever rationalizations. We blamed others and made excuses for our actions. We thought outside "conditions" had driven us to drink. It never occurred to us that WE needed to change ourselves! We also can't afford to hold back in our inventory out of shame, guilt, or pride. We needed to complete our housecleaning in order to find the "exact nature of OUR wrongs." No more half measures! Unless we were able to do this, we'd always be running from ourselves. Our entire lives we've felt threatened by so many things, and our self-centered fears consumed us. Fear was usually our first response to ANYTHING new. Learning healthy ways to acknowledge and deal with our fears, anger, resentments, and insecurities is crucial in recovery. The truth has been buried beneath layers of lies and deception. We can no longer hide behind our character defects. Today we can choose different responses. It's been said that Alcoholics Anonymous is a "great rebuilder of human wreckage." Working and reworking the steps helps us to rediscover our real selves. Recovery is all about getting something back .... OURSELVES. We are the primary beneficiary of this honest and thorough inventory.

My feelings are neither right nor wrong
but are important by virtue of being
mine."

–IN ALL OUR AFFAIRS

So many of us were out of touch with our feelings. Yet, in the course of any one day, we will find ourselves moving through a wide range of feelings. We had gotten so used to the "don't feel" rule during our addiction. When I drank, I lost touch with my feelings. I couldn't deal with them. In fact, I would do just about anything to avoid dealing with them, so I drank more! I tried ignoring my feelings by pretending they didn't exist. I also tried intellectualizing my feelings by analyzing them to death. Before I got into recovery, most of the feelings I was experiencing were negative feelings – hate, anger, shame and guilt – and had the potential to become a destructive force in my life. When they became too overwhelming for me to deal with, I simply shut down. What I had failed to see was that by not dealing with my emotions, resentments and anger, I became like a nuclear reactor ready to explode. Little did I realize back then that acceptance was often all that was needed to make them go away. But, before we can accept our feelings, we have to know what we are feeling. Feelings are like a barometer letting us know what is going on internally, helping us to navigate through life. In recovery, we give ourselves permission to feel all our emotions. There is nothing wrong with any feeling as long as they are expressed in healthy and non-abusive ways. Feelings can be amazing gifts of the program. Fear can alert us to possible danger and keep us from getting into situations that may not be in our best interest. Anger can be an incentive for us to make better choices in reclaiming our lives. Guilt can become a healthy warning device, letting us know that we crossed an unacceptable boundary. And, by experiencing sadness, we are more able to open up our heart and experience more compassion. Recovery is not about stopping the painful feelings. Getting through our painful feelings is essential for our growth. At first, it was difficult to distinguish between what we were thinking, and how we were feeling. There's a big difference. We needed to talk about our feelings. The ability to express our feelings is an important life skill. In AA we're learning to identify what we're feeling. Talking with others in the program helps. We all may have gone trough different experiences, but the feelings are the same. Going to meetings where we feel safe helps. We're here on earth to experience life, not escape from it.

• *How did you use to handle your negative feelings?*

• *What about today?*

You realize that all along there was something tremendous within you, and you did not know it. "

–PARAMAHANSA YOGANANDA

By far, the most precious gift we receive in sobriety is ourselves. The program has changed the way we view our world, our beliefs, our fears, and ultimately, ourselves. It was time for us to come back home to ourselves. I've spent most of my life looking outside myself, searching for happiness and fulfillment everywhere but within myself. Since I can remember, I've carried around the nagging feeling that something important was missing in my life. I hadn't been able to find the wonder and joy of my own existence. I felt lost, unloved and misunderstood. I was always wishing that I was some place else, or someone else, doing something different. I longed for a place where there was no trouble. I was tired of escaping through alcohol, and running away from my problems. Life will never be conflict free, and as long as we're alive, we all will have problems to work through. I needed to see that I had been creating my own unhappiness from faulty thinking. In recovery, I realize that peace and joy can be mine if I face my problems and work through the discomfort. Everything I will ever need to achieve a rich, full and sober life is already inside me. Just like the scarecrow, tin man and lion in the Wizard of Oz, we too had a heart, a mind and courage in us all along; we just weren't able to see it. All that the wizard did (just like our Higher Power) was to make everyone aware of it; he didn't give them anything they didn't already have. Dorothy even tried doing a geographic by running away, but in the end, all she wanted was to go home. Ironically, she never left her home except in her dream. She woke up in the same room where she had always been, but now she was filled with gratitude. We in AA have awakened from the nightmare of our diseased mind. We no longer need to look any farther than our own back yard. We no longer need to search over the rainbow. But how do we go about finding what we've had all along? How are we made aware of what we already know? How can we wake up to a place we've never left and the person we've always been? Simple. Join us in AA! Even though nothing has changed, everything has changed. Just like Dorothy, we are on a path of twists and turns and uncertainty with friends by our side, always taking us to a better place.

- *Where did you look for your happiness?*

- *Did you consider doing a geographic?*

- *When did you begin to look within?*

We create our fate everyday, most of the ills we suffer from are directly traceable to our own behavior."

HENRY MILLER

There were days when it seemed like everyone wanted our time, our attention and our love. Putting another person's needs ahead of our own became a daily occurrence. For years we took a back seat. For too long we've stood in the background attending to the needs of others. We were living without joy, questioning whether there was some greater source of fulfillment in store for us. The future began to look like a blank wall devoid of dreams, goals or aspirations. We had deprived and neglected ourselves for too long. That empty feeling, that sense that everyone except us has an important, valuable life, has fueled our disease for years. We seldom saw ourselves as the source of our own unhappiness, but to a large degree, it was a self-inflicted hopelessness. When I looked at my written inventory, it was revealed that my anger and resentments were really about me and my defects of character, and not about the other person at all! We can not blame our circumstances or our environment for what we have become. Had we expected our needs to be met by others? Did we neglect to care for ourselves because we were waiting for someone else to take care of us? Working the steps has empowered me and has helped me see that my well-being and happiness have always been in my own hands. I hold the key. Our recovery is dependent on our willingness to explore new ways of looking at ourselves and our lives. I am not a victim of life! If we could look at the whole picture, we'd realize that no problem ever comes to us that does not have a purpose in our lives, contributing to our inner growth. Many of us have never really learned how to take good care of ourselves, let alone others! We will be better able to be there for others when we can take care of ourselves first. We can only give what we have. If we want to have more to give to others, we must first give more to ourselves. We need to learn how to be a healthy giver. We need to be able to ask for help when we feel overwhelmed. Instead of feeling excessively responsible for others, we need to make our own well-being a priority. Self-care isn't selfish, it's self-esteem. Left untreated, it will develop into a tiredness of soul and spirit, a "soul sickness", which is a death sentence for us.

• *Do you begin to see how many of our problems were self-inflicted?*

GIVE AN EXAMPLE...

“ Fear is an insidious virus given a breeding place in our minds...it will eat away our spirit and block the forward path of our endeavors”

–James Bell

The unknown can be very frightening and can become a destructive force that overtime will disable and paralyze us from taking action. Fear becomes a power greater than ourselves, and overtime, this unrelenting fear made it difficult for us to see things in their true perspective. At its worst, fear can cause us to talk ourselves out of participating in life altogether. Fear can alter our perception of life until we lose all sense of reality. Whatever we obsess over, we empower. Whatever we fear most will be drawn to us like a magnet. We were creating mountains out of molehills. The only way to end this destructive cycle is to face our fears and then take the action by walking through them. Instead of running from our fears, we're learning to look at the source of our fears. Step 4 helps us to make an honest appraisal of where we are in our recovery. In recovery, we come to look at fear, not as a wall, but an incredible doorway of opportunity; a new beginning. On the other side of every unfamiliar door are unlimited possibilities. We needed to find the courage to step through this doorway; sometimes we just have to take a leap of faith. I've seen the world through the eyes of fear all my life. But, if we can't walk through our fears, we'll never get the chance to live our lives at all. Today stands before us waiting to be embraced, and offering so many opportunities for growth. We have to stop making excuses and rationalizations to avoid living life. Each time we face our fears we are healed, strengthened and empowered in a positive way. Each time we face one of our fears, we are a little more free. Next time you come upon a closed door, take that freeing leap of faith, or fear will be your constant companion. I've had enough of standing on the outside feeling afraid.

• *How many times have you let fear stop you from doing something you really wanted to do?*

❝ If God had wanted me otherwise, He would have created me otherwise.❞

–JOHANN VON GOETHE

In recovery we begin the task of confronting all our low self-esteem issues. We needed to examine all our behaviors – the good and the bad. They are both an integral part of who we are. Consciously or otherwise, our attitudes affect the way we perceive everything that happens in our lives. Our negative outlook caused us to see the dark side of any situation. We've carried a sense of failure and a devastated self-image around with us for years. We felt inconsequential, hardly there at all! We couldn't see how magnificent we were. No matter what wonderful things that we accomplished, it was never good enough to wipe out our flawed image of ourselves in our minds. We've struggled over the years with not feeling "normal" or not being like others. We always imagined the worst and braced ourselves for one disappointment after another. I was told that how we interpret what happens to us in life is more important than the events themselves. We can look at them as lessons in life to help us grow or we can be a victim again! For recovery to work, we need to change our self-defeating attitudes and actions. We mustn't deny, avoid, minimize, excuse or dodge any of our questionable behaviors. We can empower the problem or we can empower the solution. We have spent years negating ourselves out of existence. In recovery we're learning to be more accepting of ourselves and our imperfections, so we can be a little more comfortable in our own skin. We've also been blessed with loving, uplifting and supportive friends who love and accept us just the way we are. They see the best in us. They are able to see the human being beneath the alcoholic exterior. They see us more clearly than we can see ourselves. When those who we admire and respect treat us as worthwhile human beings, we become more receptive to positive feelings. There is so much that is right about us. We no longer define ourselves by our flaws. We're on a spiritual path of self-discovery, self-improvement and wholeness. Recovery does not mean that I have become a different person, it means I'm starting to be myself again. Today, we can approve of ourselves, and in the end, isn't this the only approval that counts? God created us in his image. Celebrate !

• *What negative thoughts that use to monopolize your thoughts, have you been able to discard for good?*

" When patterns are broken, new worlds emerge."

– TULI KUPFERBERG

Just because a decision or a choice or even a way of living was right for us yesterday, does not necessarily mean it will meet our needs or be right for us tomorrow. The time had come for us to let go of all our old ideas and beliefs that no longer worked for us. In deciding to live a clean and sober life, we would be faced with changing our entire way of living. Easier said than done! At first we dreaded all the changes we knew we would have to make in sobriety. Resistance to change is a fact of life, but we were told that if we make certain changes in our lives, we could be restored to sanity. Letting go of our old beliefs, habits, attitudes and behaviors can be very frightening and confusing. Many of us secretly wanted to go back to the way things were, where it was safe and familiar. There'll be times when we'll struggle to learn new things, and feel ill prepared for the task at hand, but we can be assured that we are in the midst of learning something important. We are going through exactly what we need to experience. We begin to see that we do have the ability to adapt to new situations, and grow beyond where we are today. In life, change is unavoidable, but it is seldom easy. And, in our case, being that we are alcoholics, change is not only desirable, but necessary. In AA we found that it would be in our own best interest to be "taken apart" and then be put back together differently. We had gotten ourselves so out of harmony with life, that we had created an energy balance that needed to be restored. AA has given us a chance to start fresh. How many people are lucky enough to get a second chance? We began to look at change as a gift, because it represented new growth.

During this time we need to be patient with ourselves and remind ourselves that we are never given more than we can handle. Stretch yourself a little more each day. What once felt overwhelming will be replaced with a quiet confi dence. Today, I can accept the changes that are occurring in my life, and I can trust that these changes are taking me to a better place of love, light and joy. We are being changed at levels deeper than we can imagine. How we fought change in the beginning!

- *What has been the most difficult change you have been faced with in sobriety?*

“ It's only by risking that we live at all.”

– WILLIAM JAMES

In the past, as a rule, I avoided life. Living life on life's terms and taking risks was just too risky! I was a "play-it-safe" kind of gal, and NOT a risk-taker. "Daring", "wild" and "impulsive" were not words I would use to define me. How unfortunate so many of us "escaped" life. We need to face life, not run or hide from it. Recovery is risky business. It involves doing things differently and trying new things. It involves going into areas that we've never been before. Why not try a new approach? Is this really such a terrible gamble? What have we got to lose? Our self-reliance had let us down again and again. All our fears had paralyzed us, leaving us feeling more separate, more alone and more afraid than ever before. Our inaction imprisoned us. We let things we couldn't do keep us from doing things we could. Our lives have the potential to be an incredible journey filled with so many wonderful experiences and "awe"-filled moments! It can be an amazing ride if we allow ourselves to remain open to all that life has to offer. We hoped our lives would change, but we took no responsibility for changing what was always in our power to change. We had so little to show for all the years when we were drinking. If we never venture forth we will never expand and grow. Taking risks and making mistakes are all part of being fully alive. In recovery, we no longer waste precious time; we begin to take calculated risks. Any new behavior requires taking risks. Life involves taking one risk after another. We make decisions and we take commitments today. These risks are worth taking; they are not the foolhardy, self-defeating risks we use to take. Sobriety doesn't just happen. We create it by finding a sponsor, going to meetings and being of service. We needed to step beyond what was comfortable. We can't wait for guarantees; we need to grab our own happiness. It's only by surviving life's experiences that we come to know who we are, what we are capable of becoming and know the strength that is available to us in every moment. The fullness of life is a natural by-product of living every day to its fullest. I don't want to live with regrets; I don't want to cheat myself out of the richness life has to off er. I have an appointment with life. Today, I am reclaiming my life. Today, I can say yes to life. Today, I can put my faith into action. Recovery is for doers. I have important things to do today. Life is a high risk proposition. The goal of recovery is to live!

• *What risks do you gladly take today?*

5

STEP FIVE

Admitted to God, to
ourselves and to another
human being the exact
nature of our wrongs

OUR SECRETS KEPT US SICK AND THEY KEPT US TRAPPED. STEP FIVE OFFERS US A WAY OUT, AND WILL GIVE US THE CLARITY WE'LL NEED FOR OUR ON-GOING SOBRIETY. MANY PEOPLE IN THE PROGRAM HAVE SHARED THAT THEY COULD NOT STAY SOBER WITHOUT DOING STEP FIVE. THIS UNBURDENING PROCESS CAN BE PAINSTAKING, BUT THE POWER OF THIS STEP CAN NOT BE IGNORED. MOST OF US DIDN'T EXACTLY LEAP AT THE OPPORTUNITY TO FACE OURSELVES. WHO WANTS THEIR PRIDE LEVELED, THEIR EGOS DEFLATED AND THEIR SHORTCOMINGS EXPOSED? WHO WANTS TO ACKNOWLEDGE ALL THE THINGS THAT THEY'VE WORKED SO HARD TO CONCEAL ALL THEIR LIVES? WE JUST KNEW DEEP DOWN THAT WE ARE ALIVE TODAY BECAUSE WE CONFRONTED ALL THE LIES AND SECRETS. WE JUST KNEW THAT WE NEEDED TO BE HONEST TO SAVE OUR LIVES. WE MUST EMBRACE THIS STEP. WE HAD TO RID OURSELVES OF ALL THE GUILT AND SHAME WE'VE CARRIED AROUND WITH US FOR SO LONG. WE NEEDED TO WALK INTO THE DARKNESS TO FIND THE LIGHT AND WALK INTO THE FEAR TO FIND PEACE OF MIND. STEP FIVE IS OUR WAY OUT OF ISOLATION AND LONELINESS. WE FOUND SOUL MATES IN AA WHO UNDERSTOOD AND GAVE US THE UNCONDITIONAL LOVE AND ACCEPTANCE WE NEEDED TO FACE OUR DEMONS. WE CAME TO SEE THAT WE WEREN'T BAD PEOPLE, ONLY SICK PEOPLE GETTING WELL. WE LEARN THAT WHAT WE'VE DONE WASN'T SO TERRIBLE OR IRREDEEMABLE AFTER ALL. OUR MISTAKES WERE NOT UNFORGIVEABLE SINS. WE HAD TO RELEASE OURSELVES FROM ALL OUR SELF-JUDGMENTS, PUNISHMENT AND GUILT THAT HAD DEFINED US FOR SO LONG. WE NEED TO RECLAIM OUR TRUE AND SPIRITUAL IDENTITY. WE BEGAN TO FORGIVE OURSELVES SO WE COULD HEAL AND CONTINUE OUR JOURNEY INTO WHOLENESS AND HAPPINESS.

"All disease comes from a state of unforgiveness."

- COURSE IN MIRACLES

What is the purpose of our recovery? Serenity? Healing? Inner peace? We came to AA so full of ourselves. But today, being at peace with ourselves is more important than getting even. Holding onto resentments is a luxury we can no longer afford to do. We will pay a high price if we refuse to forgive others and continue to nurse our grudges. Holding onto grudges makes people grumpy; they tend to scowl throughout the day. The victim, however, of any resentment is always the one who carries it. If we are not willing to forgive, there is little chance of us maintaining a sober way of living. We must not hang on to this venom of hate. Our lives should never become a breeding ground of negativity. In fact, nothing we do today will have the right outcome if we carry vengeful thoughts in our hearts. When we are consumed with revenge, there is no room for joy and love. Listing our "legitimate" complaints against those we felt had wronged us, will never get the job done. It was never our job to judge. Step Five involves the all important phase of swallowing our pride. The only inventory we need to make is our own. When I came to recognize my own irresponsible, immature, dishonest, manipulative, hypocritical, lazy self, the harder it became to criticize others. I'll leave the job of making judgment calls to others. We had to stop recycling all our old hurts over and over again in our minds. It solves nothing; there are no lessons learned. Ego and pride kill as many alcoholics as alcohol. Forgiveness is a spiritual act of love for ourselves. When we are ego-driven, we are not experiencing the sunlight of the spirit. I pray to my Higher Power to reduce the meanness in me and to help me see all the good things people do. And I pray that others be given the same healing and love that I want for myself. The spiritual way of life is not a theory. We need to live it. If we treat others with respect, courtesy and kindness, they will be more receptive to hear what we have to say. Today I seek not to condemn, but to understand. Everyday I can count my hurts or I can count my blessings. In recovery we need to nourish our minds with healthy, uplifting thoughts. I've become less judgmental as I realize that we are all travelling the same path. Let go of your hard-heartedness. Let your heart and not your ego rule your life. Our whole life will undergo an incredible change when we develop a forgiving and pardoning heart. Spiritual wellness is our goal. Give the gift of forgiveness today, and let it work its magic!

• *How has refusing to forgive someone affected your health and peace of mind?*

Relieve me of the bondage of self, that I may better do thy will."

-ALCOHOLICS ANONYMOUS

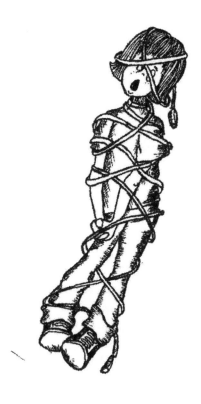

Before I sought out recovery, I couldn't see beyond myself and my need for another drink; all I ever thought about was me-me-me. I spent my days wallowing in my own selfish worries and obsessive, self-centered thoughts. My self-interests were always my priority. No one else's problems seemed as important as my own. I was consumed with all forms of "self". I was self-centered to the extreme. I was self-seeking, self-indulgent, self-absorbed, and self-righteous. I was into self-pity, self-justification, self-preservation and self-will run riot. I imposed my will to control situations and expected everyone to play by my rules. I loved getting my own way. I knew what had to be done. I had answers for everything. I rarely noticed the needs or the pain of others. So when I first arrived in Alcoholics Anonymous, no one else's problems seemed as important as my own. This non-sharing and non-caring attitude changed completely when I began working the program. Ever so slowly, I began to undo all the dysfunctional, non-productive and ineffective ways in which I had dealt with life. I am no longer the center of the universe. Recovery is all about getting back a healthy sense of ourselves. Our need for excessive attention is redirected. In AA we begin to look beyond ourselves. Something far greater than ourselves has taken root. We learn about humility and the complete freedom from ourselves that it teaches. We begin to recognize that other people's problems are just as important as our own. Frequent contact with the newcomer becomes the bright spot in our lives. Their pain and frustration are every bit as real as our own. The world no longer revolves around me. Self-forgetting is key. "Thy will be done" becomes more than mere words. Loving, caring, sharing – that's what Sobriety is all about. We need to make room for others in our lives. For those still struggling alone, the remedy is as close as another alcoholic. When a newcomer arrives, we widen the circle. The loving hands of AA will always be there. We've been given a second chance at a worthwhile life. We've been restored to sanity and the promises are being fulfi lled. After being such a taker all my life, being able to experience the joy of pure giving becomes a life-changing experience. How ironic that my pain had become the healing balm for another. Today I cherish the security of love returned. Let others into your life.

• *What does "relieved of bondage" mean to you?*

" We are only as sick as the secrets we keep."

–SUE ATCHLEY EBAUGH

Our illness was amazingly difficult to see from the outside because we wore a mask of wellness and success to win the acceptance of others. What we were truly feeling on the inside rarely showed up on the outside. Our hearts could be breaking, but we kept on smiling. Beneath our masks were closely guarded secrets. We lived our lives without anyone ever really getting to know us. We were very selective in choosing what we wanted others to know about us. Our alcoholism has resulted in a lifetime of secrets causing us to be silent rather than honest. Our embarrassing secrets kept us stuck in shame. We suffered in silence fearing what others would think if they knew the truth! These burdens weighed heavily on us. We began to think that our self-worth was beyond repair and that our lives would never be any different. We hated this disease and ourselves for making us feel so different from everyone else. This addiction robbed us of our dignity and self-respect and drained our lives of vitality, joy and meaning. Step Five is an important part of the recovery process for those of us who have learned to keep secrets. We were told that we are only as sick as our secrets. And I was sick! I had to come out of hiding. I could no longer hide behind this mask of wellness. Once and for all I had to breakdown the walls I had built up around my secret world of addiction. In AA we are shown a way out of our dark, secret world with total self-disclosure. Just as denial had made my addiction work, rigorous honesty is what will make my recovery work. In order to live, I had to confront the lies. I knew I would have to start getting honest in every area of my life. There's nothing more difficult to do than facing ourselves as we really are. In meetings we hear others in recovery share their darkest and most distressing thoughts and inner most fears with painstaking honesty without fear of rejection, judgment, or disapproval. This honesty opened up the door for others to share as well. Removing the mask becomes the starting point for our recovery. Today we understand that we are good people who have just been sick. Each day since, we are fi nding it easier to live in the real world. We've removed the mask. Once upon a time, my life was a complicated lie. I have no secrets today. The truth has set me free!

• *What fears arose when you admitted the exact nature of your wrongs?*

Rejection?

Disapproval?

Abandonment?

"The art of life lies in a constant re-adjustment to our surroundings."

–OKAKURA KAKUZO

How often have we mistakenly thought we had everything under control, and then got broadsided by reasons and circumstances beyond our control that we never bargained for? One of the most important life skills we'll acquire in sobriety is our ability to adapt to unexpected situations so we can experience life more fully. We use to be so stubborn and inflexible which had created enormous stress in us. As addictive and compulsive people we know a lot about extremes and very little about moderation. Anything we can do, we can under do or over do. One of the things we strive for in recovery is balance – that "precious middle ground". In recovery we begin to move away from extremes in order to find this balance. In the past, I lived in extremes. I did everything in excess. I drank too much. I cried too much. I blamed too much. I tolerated too much or too little. I was either thinking of others without a single thought of myself, or I was completely self-obsessed. I felt terribly inferior or arrogantly superior. I allowed demands of family, job and children to consume me. I was compulsive, obsessive and an over-achiever. Many of us were workaholics and were all work and no play, and others of us were all play and no work. We were either straining to retain total control over our lives, or we took absolutely no responsibility for our lives. The purpose of Step Five is to help us accept the truth about the ways we've reacted to people, places and things in our lives. We use to view solutions as a change that needed to occur in other people and never within ourselves. Recovery requires a shift in the ways we think and act. Recovery brings balance back into our lives, bringing with it much needed perspective and wisdom. I've finally realized that I can't prepare for life; it will always take me unaware. For reasons outside our control, situations can change and turn into something we never bargained for. No matter what chaos is going on around us, maintaining balance between what we can and can't change becomes a way of life. It does no good to stubbornly hold on to something that isn't working anymore. Because a decision was right yesterday, doesn't mean it will meet our needs tomorrow. Balance is the key to a long and healthy life. The person who has achieved this inner peace has found the key to right living. For most of my life I felt there just weren't enough hours in a day. I set impossible goals for myself. Today I'm emotionally and physically available to others and have become a constant and stable presence in my own life and the life of my family. Life is daily and I need to fi nd balance. In fl exibility lies great strength.

• *What extreme actions led you to the brink of insanity or relapse?*

• *How do you find balance today?*

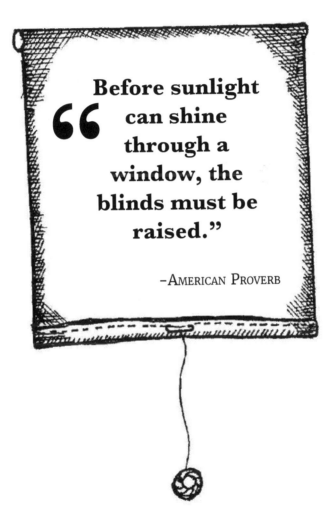

Before sunlight can shine through a window, the blinds must be raised."

–AMERICAN PROVERB

Before we arrived in Alcoholics Anonymous, we had experienced a prolonged and painful withdrawal from life. Somewhere along the way we lost ourselves and journeyed into darkness. We were in a never-ending flight from life. We weren't living; we were dying. Our hearts had been filled with so much darkness, that we couldn't find the joy in our own existence. Before choosing recovery, our lives were like a boarded-up house. We had pulled down the shades, drew the curtains, closed the shutters, bolted the door, unplugged the phones and proceeded to drink all alone for years. We were living our lives stumbling around in the darkness for years. Our first reaction to this disease was to hide it. We've spent years working very hard to conceal all our shameful secrets, harmful resentments and paranoid fears that have weighed so heavily on us. We were too frightened to live in the present, and we were too shamed by our past. We would have done just about anything to avoid looking at ourselves. For many of us it was so much easier to shut down, rather than open up. As our disease progressed, our world continued to grow smaller and narrower. In order to heal from this disease we had to do extensive, internal housecleaning. The house (our lives) had suffered from years of neglect. The interior was stale and dusty, showing signs of decay. It was time to sweep out the cobwebs and demons, raise the blinds and open the windows and doors to let fresh air and sunlight in. We had to risk exposing our innermost selves to get rid of all that's been holding us back. It's not enough to look at only the parts we liked. We needed to look at all the things we'd rather forget. Life is a package deal. We needed to unlock all the secrets of our past. We needed to remove all the guilt and shame, the unhealed memories and all the unresolved feelings. We can't whitewash new paint over the decay. What's old and decayed must be removed. We needed to begin to build a new foundation based on honesty. We needed to make room for all our talents and strengths. Our lives should be a journey of joyful discoveries. Little by little, we're learning to risk revealing who we really are. We had been preoccupied with sheer survival. In recovery we are given the opportunity to begin searching for greater meaning, purpose and deeper fulfillment in our lives. We've embarked on an amazing journey of self-discovery. We're learning a new way of living that is very different from the way we've ever approached life before. Exploring and embracing our dark side is the only way we can truly live in the light. The dark part of our lives that held no promise or future is behind us. In Step Five we've opened the doors and windows of our lives to reveal our true selves. Our goal in recovery is to live. Say yes to life!

- *Have you begun your housecleaning?*

- *What treasures have you uncovered?*

66 **The worst thing you can do is to try to cling to something that's gone, or try to re-create it."**

–JOHNETTE NAPOLITANO

W e needed to say good-bye to the past and let the healing begin. The time had come for us to once and for all let go of all our old ways of living that were no longer taking us where we needed to go. They no longer represented the person we were striving to become. All those tried and true behaviors that had once allowed us to function in the past, have now become obstacles to our growth and recovery. I had the hardest time letting go of the past. Letting go of my old habits was like letting go of a valued friend who had helped me cope and feel safe when nothing else did.

OUR PAST WILL ALWAYS BE A PART OF US AND FACING IT IS AN IMPORTANT PART OF THE HEALING PROCESS.

I needed to remain open to what was coming next, rather than clinging to the way things were. Being available and open to the present is our best opportunity for positive change and healthy growth. When we cling to the past, we become unavailable to the present. We can't allow the past to hold us back from living any longer. Each new day offers us opportunities to let go of all that has trapped us in the past. We had brought a lot of baggage and unfinished business with us when we got here. We needed to start each day with a clean slate. We had to let go of yesterday and let tomorrow take care of itself. We need to take each day as it comes. Living in the moment gives us the strength to follow through every day. It is the daily living that gives us the satisfaction to get on with our lives. Our lives are ever-changing. No one can predict what the next change will be or what unexpected treasures and opportunities await us. Sometimes the unexpected is far better than anything we could have planned. This program has given us a chance to make a brand new start. I no longer want to drag my past into the future. I came to AA because I was ready to heal. The past does not exist anymore, but we must never look back with regret or wish to shut the door on it. We need to be grateful for all the lessons it taught us. Ironically, the past has become our most valuable and prized possession. The past becomes the key, not the lock to the future. Lighter times are coming. Be ready to welcome them with open arms.

- *What were some of your old survival skills?*

"We would have to settle for the elegant goal of becoming ourselves."

–WILLIAM STYRON

W e've carried a sense of inadequacy around with us all our lives. We only saw lack and limitation. We were always putting ourselves down for not having enough or being enough. Everyone else always seemed so self-assured and confident. They seemed to always have it all together. When they made mistakes, their self-esteem remained intact. If we had only found the right clothes, the right college, the right job, the right car, the right house or the right friends, we could have been someone special too. So much of my life seemed to be based on trying to impress others by buying things I really didn't need, with money I really didn't have, to impress people I really didn't like. But no matter how intelligent and attractive we may have been, as alcoholics we doubted our worthiness. We had trouble permitting ourselves to be just as flawed as everyone else. One of life's unavoidable lessons is that we'll never be able to please all the people all the time. We will never be able to win the approval of everyone we meet. To recover we needed to be accepting of who we are now. People will love us and others will hate us, and none of it has anything to do with us! Step Five is the antidote to being stuck in an unhealthy state of mind. Step Five is a true exercise in humility. We work this step by being honest – rigorously honest. We see ourselves so differently today. We're finally learning to distinguish the person from the disease. What's important to me has changed in sobriety. The true measure of success in life does not come down to what we do or how we look, but from how much love we carry inside our hearts. Discovering our unconditional human worth has provided a foundation from which we can build a new and sober life. Self-love has taken root and has become a positive and guiding force in our lives today. The best thing I can do for my continuing sobriety is to simply be myself. We had to stop focusing on our imperfections, insisting that things should be other than they are. We had to stop wanting to change ourselves and think more about accepting ourselves.

**IF WE TRY TO BE LIKE EVERYONE ELSE, WE WILL
ALWAYS BE AN UNAUTHENTIC SECOND BEST.**

- *What about you gives you the greatest joy today?*

- *What about you makes your spirit come alive?*

FOCUS ON THAT!

6

STEP SIX

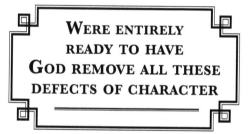

WERE ENTIRELY READY TO HAVE GOD REMOVE ALL THESE DEFECTS OF CHARACTER

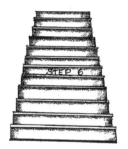

OUR INCREASING DESIRE TO HEAL AND GROW HAS BROUGHT US TO STEP SIX– THE LAST PREPARATION STEP. THE INTERNAL CHANGES WE ARE EXPERIENCING IS A GROWING READINESS AND WILLINGNESS TO HAVE GOD REMOVE OUR CHARACTER DEFECTS. WE INVITE GOD INTO OUR LIVES AND ALLOW HIM TO WORK THROUGH US TO CHANGE OUR LIVES. OUR PAST HAS BEEN DOMINATED BY OUR STRONG SELF-WILL. OUR LIVES HAD BECOME SO UNMANAGEABLE, THAT CHANGING OUR BEHAVIORS BECAME OUR ONLY OPTION NEXT TO INSANITY OR DEATH. WE HAD REACHED THE POINT IN OUR DRINKING, WHEN WE COULD NO LONGER FIGHT, MANIPULATE, CHEAT, BEG, BORROW OR STEAL OUR WAY OUT OF ALL THE MISTAKES WE MADE WHEN DRINKING. WE REALIZED THAT OUR OLD COPING BEHAVIORS, SURVIVAL SKILLS AND ALL OUR DYSFUNCTIONAL, NON-PRODUCTIVE AND INEFFECTIVE WAYS OF DEALING WITH LIFE THAT ONCE PROTECTED US WERE NOW GETTING IN THE WAY OF THE NEW LIFE WE WANTED FOR OURSELVES. BUT RECOGNIZING THIS NEED FOR CHANGE, AND ACTUALLY CHANGING OUR LIVES ARE TWO VERY DIFFERENT THINGS! THIS READINESS FOR CHANGE ONLY IMPLIES OUR ACCEPTANCE OF THINGS AS THEY REALLY ARE. WHEN WE TRULY WANT CHANGE, LASTING CHANGE, MUCH MORE WORK LIES AHEAD OF US. THESE CHANGES DO NOT HAPPEN OVERNIGHT. WE'RE NOT JUST LETTING GO OF OUR CHARACTER DEFECTS, BUT OF AN ENTIRE WAY OF LIFE. GENUINE SOBRIETY CAN ONLY BE ATTAINED THROUGH PROFOUND CHANGES IN EVERY AREA OF OUR LIVES. TODAY I USE THE STRENGTH, LOVE AND WISDOM OF A POWER GREATER THAN MYSELF. WE ARE NOT THE ONES DOING THE REMOVING. GOD REMOVES THESE DEFECTS. IT'S OUR JOB TO BECOME ENTIRELY READY. THE REWARDS FROM WORKING THIS STEP WILL BE PEACE AND SERENITY EACH TIME WE COMPLETE A TASK THAT WAS ONCE DIFFICULT TO FACE. WE HAD TO FIND THE WILLINGNESS TO BE UNCOMFORTABLE. WE NEEDED TO GET RID OF THE OLD TO MAKE ROOM FOR THE NEW. READINESS IS THE KEY.

" True happiness is a by-product of an effort to make someone else happy."

–Gretta Brooker Palmer

How many of us are truly happy? There seems to be so many unhappy people in the world. Surely God did not want us to live our lives in misery, moping around and feeling blue. Everyone wants to be happy, but there were so many of us who just didn't know where or how to find it. When I first arrived in AA, I truly felt that I had absolutely nothing to offer anyone. I was an empty shell of a human being, desperately wanting to fill up the hole inside me with something to make me feel better, feel alive. I used to look for happiness in self-centered ways and invested time and energy in materialistic "things". Why wasn't I as happy as I ought to be? I found that the kind of happiness that comes from "getting" is shallow and only gave me fleeting moments of happiness, at best. Takers can never be really happy. We can't buy happiness either. Many of us had to redefine what true happiness is. We've learned, usually the hard way that the things we thought we wanted didn't bring happiness after all. When I began to go to meetings, something touched me. I saw pain and sadness transformed into joy and serenity. I witnessed others giving of themselves without expecting anything in return. The feelings everyone shared came from their hearts, and there were smiles and there was laughter. I began to relate, and I knew at that moment that I wanted what they had. I kept coming back. My life began to change. In AA, we put love into action, blessing both the giver and the receiver. The experience of loving is reward in itself. Ironically, the more love we give, the more love we find within ourselves to give. If we feel good about ourselves, we'll create happiness wherever we go, but first we had to get rid of the negativity, the worries and the resentments. Real happiness for me is extending my hand to someone else in need, touching their heart. Everyday we have an opportunity to make someone feel a little better. Today I'm filled with a desire to help others and be of service. When love fills your life, all limitations disappear. The medicine this sick world needs so badly is love. Giving attention by sharing our experiences, hopes and stories is the key to finding real happiness. Truly being there for one another brings happiness. Happiness is the result of right actions. Be the reason someone smiles today. Be a rainbow in someone else's cloud today.

• *What brings you happiness today?*

" *It's the steady constant driving to the goals for which you're striving, not the speed with which you travel that will make your victory sure.*"

– ANONYMOUS

Headstrong and full of self-will, our lives had been devoted to pursuing self-centered desires. We pretty much did as we pleased and went where and when the spirit moved us. We were running in circles getting nowhere fast. We lacked goals and our lives were unfocused and disorganized. Recovery is far to important to leave to chance. We needed to develop the discipline to take responsibility for our lives and stay with it no matter what. Change won't happen until we commit to it. Discipline isn't easy or fun, but it's the best friend we'll have in early recovery. Persistence, determination and commitment become our greatest assets when used properly. It's the daily striving, not the occasional striving that will make our recovery strong, or all that we've gained may be lost. Our character defects have been deeply ingrained in us over the years of daily struggling. We need time to work through our problems, assimilate new ideas and make crucial life-affirming, lifestyle changes. Sobriety is all about the journey. There is no such thing as standing still in recovery. We do nothing and this disease gets worse. Sobriety is a lifelong undertaking. Even after years in AA, this disease is still very much alive and well in us. We're up against a formidable opponent that is not going to give up without a fight. On this journey we'll move forward and backwards. We'll take detours and even lose our way from time to time. But we'll always find our way back as long as we work the program daily. Our Higher Power will help us negotiate the twists and turns of the journey ahead of us. Step Six is all about our growing willingness and readiness to trust in God's timetable. We are becoming ready to know a new freedom. Little by little, our lives began to work, and all the weeks and months of blind faith were beginning to pay off. I might not see many results today, but I can trust in the progress I'm making. There is no such as being late. The time it takes is the time that is needed. In AA we don't give up. We know that nothing is less important than the score at half-time. We need to let our recovery unfold at its own pace. We should not be in such a hurry to move on. We're not in a race. It's not where we came from or even where we are now, but it's where we are headed that matters. We take the program with us wherever we go. *Don't quit 5 minutes before the miracle! Our lives have purpose and direction today.*

- *Which character defects continue to interfere with your progress?*

❝❝ *Men will get no more out of life than they put into it."*

– WILLIAM J.H. BOETCKER

How often have you laid around wishing for a better life? The program of Alcoholics Anonymous is a plan for a lifetime of daily living. AA offers us an extraordinary opportunity to improve the quality of our lives. In the past, we fantasized about the life we wished we were living. We explored endless possibilities to make our lives better and then did absolutely nothing to make it a reality. It's been said that the tragedy of life is not that it ends so soon, but that we waited so long to begin it! We shouldn't believe also that our best days exist somewhere "out there" in the future. We needed to do more than wishful thinking and daydreaming about improving the quality of our lives. In recovery, it was time that we made a positive contribution to our own well-being. We've barely scratched the surface of our talents and abilities. Don't settle for where you are in life today without a dream to reach for. We've let so many dreams die in the past. The good news is that there are no expiration dates on dreams. I want to enthusiastically greet each day with a desire to live my life to the fullest. Let go of all your excuses. Perseverance is not the least bit interested in our excuses! It's all about following through on what we said we were going to do. Step Six is the Step we needed to work that will enable us to change the course of our lives. We've recognized the need to change, now we needed to develop the willingness. Willingness will be the state of mind that will propel us into action. Today my life is built upon little, everyday accomplishments. These actions have allowed me to break out of my unhealthy patterns of the past. Setting goals and taking small risks has become a daily striving to make my life better. Once the plan is set in motion, action becomes the magic word. We can't afford to drift into complacency or indifference. Don't put off until tomorrow all the things that are crying for our attention today. We can't think our way into a beautiful life. Action is what makes the difference. If we aren't giving life all we've got, then we are not living up to all we can be. Sobriety is not for people who need it, but for people who want it and will go to any lengths to get it. We just have this one life to live. We owe it to ourselves to experience all that life has to offer. The real gifts of sobriety will be beyond our reach if we choose inaction. How many of us have lived up to our potential?

• *What things have you enthusiastically talked about doing, but never got around to doing?*

"We've been doing the wrong things for all the right reasons."

–Co-Dependent No More

By the time I reached Step Six, I was exhausted. I felt like I had been put through the wringer, especially after completing my Fourth Step inventory. Who wants to look at their character defects and deal with the possibility of disapproval and rejection? I was drowning in my own pain and powerlessness. To get the validation, sense of identity, love and relief that I craved, I turned to caretaking. Caretaking fulfilled a tremendous need in me for love and acceptance at a time when I felt so unlovable. I wanted to "fix" everything and everybody. I became neurotically needy. By taking care of others, especially my children, I began to feel better about myself. I told myself that I was filling a need by protecting them from all the pain of living life on life's terms. But, it is not my job to solve other people's problems. I knew that as much as I wanted to protect my family from all the pain and discomfort of living, I realized it was wrong. No longer do I do things for others that they can and should be doing for themselves. They must learn to be accountable for their own actions and find their own way in the world. I had robbed them of a sense of achievement. I need to remember to give those I love the right to make their own mistakes. They have to learn how to help themselves. What I can do is to love and guide them, and provide a nurturing and safe environment for them in which to grow strong. I had focused all my attention where it didn't belong. Recovery is all about letting go of all the things we couldn't change. The bottom line is that I can't change other people, solve their problems or control their behaviors. Real power lies in the wisdom to know the difference. Though I "rescued" others out of love, I ended up not only shortchanging them, but myself as well. Healing begins when we become aware of how we had attempted to use others to stop our pain. Today, I'm learning how to give to others in healthy ways. Someone once pointed out to me that if you feed a down- and- out man a meal, you've fed him for one day, but if you teach this man how to grow food, he'll have enough food for a lifetime.

• *In the past, did you practice caretaking?*

• *In taking care of everyone else, what important things did you neglect doing for yourself ?*

"The greatest gift I can give myself is my own attention."

–Anonymous

How many times have we used other people's problems as an excuse to avoid looking at our own? Over the years, it became more and more necessary for me to escape from myself. Discounting myself by minimizing all my achievements, feelings and needs was all I knew how to do. Because I had such a low opinion of myself and was filled with so much shame, I focused on everyone else's "stuff". I would do just about anything to draw attention away from myself. So many of us came to AA appearing opinionated, self-righteous, unique and arrogant, but underneath, we were just plain scared, feeling "not enough", insecure and very lonely. Forming meaningful relationships was so difficult for most of us. We longed to have the intimacy that "normal" people seemed to develop over time. We desperately wanted to win the approval and acceptance of others. But, this disease is one of self-centeredness, and unfortunately, when the ego gets involved, we usually switch back over to our attack and destroy mode. We've spent a lifetime trying to be right by making everyone else wrong. It may have built up our fragile egos temporarily, but it came with a high price – it was at the expense of someone else. Gossip is character assassination, and is a form of control that grows out of our insecurities. I needed to control others to feel secure, and I used it to blame, destroy, express anger and find fault with others. But in the end, all it had accomplished was to diminish myself – the exact opposite of what I wanted! One goal in recovery is to discover real intimacy and to form relationships that work. Both gossip and intimacy are ways to connect with others – one is destructive, the other, constructive. Gossip blocks any chance of true intimacy. In recovery, we need to focus on ourselves – the good and the bad. The only inventory

I need to begin to take is my own. Our feelings are valid and important. We do count. Find your voice. Self-assurance will gradually replace our self-doubts. I'm not use to admitting my wrongs and mistakes, but, I'm learning to do things that make me feel better about myself, rather than looking good to others. AA has given me something of real value that I can share with others. We've bee given the tools of honesty and humility. Today, I'm free and secure enough to trust and be trusted, and to give and receive real love. We all want to leave a lasting impression that we leave behind. For me, I hope it is for the honesty I try to demonstrate, the patience I try to live by and the compassion I feel for others.

- *Have you ever used gossip to look better in someone else's eyes ?*

- *How did it make you feel afterwards?*

- *Did it promote self-esteem?*

remember...

T
R
U
S
T

TAKES

YEARS TO BUILD

SECONDS TO BREAK

&

FOREVER TO REPAIR !

A part of me wants to cling to old resentments, but I know that the more I forgive, the better my life works."

—In all Our Affairs

Even after being in the program a while, I still may feel an overwhelming desire to get even; I still want revenge. But today, being at peace with myself, and the world, is more important than getting even. I had been a slave to negative behaviors, justifiable resentments, judgmental thoughts, self-righteous self-pity and false pride. Today, I'm open to the lessons my feelings are trying to teach me, so I can make positive and constructive changes in my life. I use to blame others for how I felt, but I can no longer allow anger and resentments to build up in me until they explode in inappropriate ways at inopportune times! Thoughts of revenge only postpone my dealing with the real and painful feelings underneath my resentments. All my negative emotions had stunted my spiritual growth and put distance between me and others. Revenge may have given me a temporary feeling of satisfaction, but I needed to ask myself, "is attacking someone going to help me solve my problems?" Negative thinking is a luxury I can no longer afford to be a part of. (It's like drinking poison and expecting the other person to die!) Learning new and respectful ways to respond when I'm angry is a positive sign of recovery. I needed to learn how to express my feelings honestly, respectfully and assertively. Forgiveness may be the greatest healer of them all. When I'm not in a forgiving frame of mind, my life suffers. We can either focus on all that's wrong or we can look for the good that can come out of any situation. I've chosen to use my painful experiences to make a positive difference with a message of hope. When we are taking good care of ourselves, we don't need our defects of character to function. We've been given a daily reprieve from our disease contingent upon our spiritual condition. There can be no spirituality without loving kindness. The key to Step Six is that God removes these character defects. It's our job to become entirely ready. In Step 6 we invite God into our lives. This Step involves a willingness on our part to allow God to work through us to change our lives. We behave the way we believe God wants us to behave. We need to nourish our minds with healthy thoughts. We need to associate with people who inspire us, believe in us and provides us with positive encouragement and support. Let go of any residual resentments. We've been so caught up in our own troubles that we were unable to see the higher purpose of our lives.

• *How do you respond when someone around you is negative or critical towards you?*

• *Do you harbor a resentment?*

• *Do you ever consider the possibility that they may have had a bad day?*

• *Have you tried forgiveness?*

"AA is designed to secure the greatest possible inner security for us long-time escapists. The feeling of impending disaster begins to dissolve."

–THE GRAPEVINE

So much of our anxiety and fearfulness stemmed from the belief that we couldn't live life on life's terms. But as we grew in the program, we started to see our world differently. The memories of our painful past are subsiding as we begin to grow in our relationship with our Higher Power. We've worked hard at developing more faith. It's easy to speak of faith, but it's quite another matter to actually live it. Faith takes practice, patience and courage. Our fears have loomed large in our minds, and it takes courage to step beyond what is comfortable and known. We've spent years trying to safeguard our lives. For years I sat on the sidelines watching my life pass me by, feeling more and more disconnected from life. What's important is that we put one foot in front of the other and move forward. Recovery involves doing what we need to do in spite of fear. We can't be so afraid of life. Faith is about taking action. Our alcoholism robbed us of an active life. The real gifts of sobriety will be beyond our reach if we choose inaction. Faith is believing that someone or something will take care of us and carry us through terribly confusing times. Faith is giving up control of the outcomes from our actions. Faith is not having to have all the answers. Faith is believing that even in bad times, all is good. Faith is no longer waiting for the other shoe to drop. Faith is knowing that God is alive in our choices. My faith has enabled me to change. Uncertainty need not be terrifying. In recovery we are taken beyond our problems that once held us captive in a constant state of nameless fears. There will be problems, and we may not know what's coming next, but we will get through them. The arrival of faith in our lives has been gradual, and each day offers us the opportunity to build up a supply of positive experiences. We begin to feel secure in the knowledge of God's love and perfect plan for our lives. Peace and serenity are not reached by the absence of conflict, but by the presence of a Higher Power in our daily lives. Today I will take note of what happens when I trust my Higher Power, and how much easier my day is when I leave the outcome where it belongs. Today faith and courage come together to get the job done. Trusting is a key part of recovery. Being in AA is like stepping into a bright new world.

• *What baby steps did you take since you first entered the program to ease your fear of the unknown?*

• *What changes have you noticed in your behavior?*

7

Step Seven

Humbly asked Him to remove our shortcomings

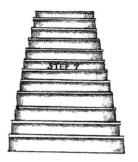

WE WERE A DISASTER WAITING TO HAPPEN. OUR SELF-WILLS WERE ALWAYS PUTTING US INTO SOME SORT OF COLLISION COURSE WITH SOMEONE OR SOMETHING. OUR PAST, WITH ALL ITS PAIN AND INSANITY, HAS FINALLY CAUGHT UP TO US. OUR LIVES WERE FALLING APART. BY STEP SEVEN, WE'VE LET GO OF THE ILLUSION THAT WE COULD RUN OUR OWN LIVES. WE FELT HELPLESS TO CHANGE OUR LIVES, AS WE BECAME HUMBLED BY THIS DISEASE. THE TIME HAD COME FOR HUMBLE PRAYER. BY ACCEPTING THE FACT THAT GOD CAN DO FOR US WHAT WE COULD NOT, WE BEGAN TO ACQUIRE THE HUMILITY THAT WAS NECESSARY FOR REAL AND LASTING CHANGE TO TAKE PLACE. WE NEEDED TO ACCEPT OUR HUMAN LIMITATIONS. IT'S THE FIRST TIME WE ASK GOD DIRECTLY FOR HIS HELP; STEP SEVEN WAS A GENUINE CRY FOR HELP. (IN THE PAST, GOD WAS USUALLY OUR LAST RESORT.) IN RECOVERY WE DEVELOP A WILLINGNESS TO ALLOW GOD TO WORK THROUGH US. WITHOUT FREEDOM FROM ALCOHOL WE HAVE NOTHING, AND WE CAN'T BE FREE OF OUR ADDICTION UNTIL WE DEAL WITH OUR CHARACTER DEFECTS WHICH HAVE BROUGHT US TO OUR KNEES IN PRAYER. EVERYWHERE WE SAW FAILURE AND MISERY TRANSFORMED. WHO EVER THOUGHT THAT HUMILITY WOULD BRING US THE STRENGTH TO RISE ABOVE OUR PAST FAILURES AND BECOME THE HEALER OF OUR PAIN? WE SURRENDER TO THIS POWER EVERYDAY. WE TRULY ARE IN HIS LOVING CARE.

**"Great people are just
ordinary people with an
extraordinary amount of
determination"**

–ROBERT SCHULLER

Most of our lives have been devoted to fulfilling our self-centered desires. Most of us fail, not because we lack talent or opportunity, but because we don't give life all we've got. When tough times come and situations look hopeless, do we wallow in self-pity, panic inside, pack up and quit? I've tried controlling situations and forcing desired outcomes for years. All my life I've been told that if I put my mind to anything I wanted, I would manifest it. I usually proceeded full speed ahead. Until I got what I wanted, there was nothing that would stop me. For years this worked out well for me, especially in maintaining my supply of alcohol. My priority became anything that would ease my intolerable pain and shame. Alcohol became an insatiable need that could never be satisfied. I was in the grips of an addictive process more powerful than me. It had become a craving more important than life itself! I'm one of the strongest willed persons I know, but my incredible strength of will was not enough to save my life. After years of trying, my strong will hadn't made my situation any better. To be honest, it made a bad situation so much worse. It nearly cost me my life. I can't remember how many times I got my own way and lived to regret it! I had a strong will, but it was the wrong kind of will. Now, in recovery, I can use this same stubborn determination to honor my commitment to the program to maintain my sobriety. Today, I don't drink - no matter what! Today I'm setting new priorities. In recovery, our energies are being redirected, but with the same focused intent, unfailing concentration and persistent willingness. There will be times when serenity will elude us, and leave us feeling disconnected from our Higher Power. We may even feel like we've lost our way and nothing seems to help. When this happens, we go to more meetings, call our sponsor more often, journal and even pray and meditate more. Sometimes, sobriety is just putting one foot in front of the other and doing what we need to do to get through the day, hour or minute. If we can hold on and keep working our program, these tough times will pass. We all have hopes and plans for the future. Dream your dreams. Put all you've got into whatever you're doing. Win or lose, succeed or fail, go for it! Everything was, is, and always will be in God's capable hands. How utterly powerless I was to change my own life! I still think of the insanity of this disease and where it took me. I no longer impose my will. Today I'm willing to place God's will above my own willful nature.

• *When things seem hopeless and beyond repair, what actions do you take to insure your sobriety?*

" The day is lost on which one has not laughed."

– FRENCH PROVERB

One of the most overlooked and underrated gifts of sobriety is the gift of laughter. Laughter was sorely missing in our lives, but it became the magic ingredient in our recovery. We all need laughter in our lives. We use to be in so much pain. We knew only too well the sorrow, the struggles and the despair of this disease. Before recovery laughter was one of the most painful sounds we knew. We had to find a way to replace our weariness of spirit with joy and positive thoughts. We need to be able to see the lighter side of life. Laughter has a way of putting everything in perspective. Laughter has great curative properties. When laughter returns it begins to recharge every cell in our bodies. We need to be able to laugh instead of complain. We can never eliminate all the negativity in our lives, but we can dilute it with positive thoughts. Recovery is all about giving ourselves permission to be human. With each pratfall we become more human. It allows us to express self-forgiveness for our imperfections. When I could finally laugh at myself, I knew I was changing and growing in self-esteem. Today I can risk being embarrassed realizing how easy it is to recover. When I could finally laugh at myself, I knew I was being restored to sanity. I had almost forgotten how good it felt to laugh again. Best of all, laughter is contagious. It multiplies each time it's shared! The Big Book says we are not "a glum lot". We can have fun, be spontaneous and let ourselves feel the good feelings. We need to enjoy, cherish and celebrate our recovery. As we grow in the program and begin to work through our problems, we are able to make more room for laughter. It is the best pain reliever I know of today. What was once the most painful sound I knew, has now become music to my ears. Stay close to others in the program who laugh easily and often. Get into the habit of laughing. Too many of us have forgotten how. Let laughter become your spiritual tonic for the day. Spread happiness and laughter everywhere you go. Give it as a gift to others. Life is too important to be taken too seriously!

• *What are some of the things you do to have fun today without drinking?*

• *Are you able to laugh at yourself today?*

I care not what others think of what I do, but I care very much about what I think of what I do. That's character."

- TEDDY ROOSEVELT

I've spent too much time feeling badly about who I am, and what I've done over the years. For too many years, because of my addiction, I couldn't love myself. I have spent most of my life feeling inadequate and unattractive. My identity was bound up in a knot of shame. All my attempts at self-love always seemed to fall short when I measured them against others. I was always minimizing my own needs, feelings, opinions, achievements and even my goals and dreams. As a result, I had desperately looked outside myself for approval. Self-love was a new behavior for most of us, but it was a crucial element in our recovery. I came into Alcoholics Anonymous feeling like a "nobody", and wanting so badly to be a "somebody", but by then I thought my self-esteem was beyond repair. Before I came to AA, I didn't believe I made mistakes, I believed I was a mistake. There's a big difference! But because of working the steps, I no longer allow my problems and mistakes to define who I am. Today, I realize my self-worth is not dependant on the approval of others; it truly is an inside job. I had blocked my own well-being each time I based my self-worth on what others thought of me. I needed to begin to make choices that would allow me to feel good about myself. Today, I'm working at developing new behaviors that reflect my new found integrity and spiritual growth. I began to do estimable things, and I began to like the person I saw in the mirror. All of us can improve our lives by simply doing loving things that we know how to do. I give what I have today. When I take responsibility for my actions and my life, regardless of what other people do or say, I'm becoming someone I can be proud of. Because of the program, I'm finding the courage to be true to myself, whether or not others agree with me. No one can make my life wonderful but me. We're so fortunate to have this program that has given us the opportunity to help one another as we help ourselves grow in love. I embrace the steps today and I take the program with me everywhere I go. AA has filled my days with loving and caring friends, genuine and light-hearted laughter and new feelings of self-worth. My life is so different today. It's as if I have been given a new pair of glasses. Today, I know I'm doing the best I can. I am all that I need to be and more. A new confidence and faith have entered my life, and I have hope to share and love to give. The focus today is on me. My ego and pride have been replaced with gratitude for the miracle of recovery. We've begun to live our lives with integrity and purpose.

•*How did you begin to rebuild your self-esteem?*

•*What things have you done to be proud of?*

Do I realize that by resenting someone, I allow that person to live rent free in my head?"

— A Day At a Time

Was serenity beyond our reach? Do we really want to continue to carry toxic grudges around with us? This negativity is so dangerous to our on-going sobriety. Without forgiveness, our resentments will continue to undermine all our growth and progress that we've worked so hard on. Without forgiveness in our hearts, the quality of our sobriety will suffer greatly. Many of us have gone through life with a long list of hurts, traumas and injustices that we've dragged around with us wherever we went. If we leave these feelings unresolved, they will drive us back to our addiction in a heartbeat, keeping us tied to an unending cycle of anger and bitterness. The irony is that we can't punish anyone without punishing ourselves in the process. We are the ones who ultimately have to live with all the negative fallout it produces. It handcuffs us to the person we believed had "wronged us" and leaves us dependent on the other person to change for our lives to improve. In blaming others, we are giving away our power. The anger that it produces is directed back at us. Getting into recovery is our opportunity for spiritual growth, but it is very difficult to be spiritually fit and full of love if we harbor these toxic feelings. We've been told in AA that if we hold onto any resentment, we need to look within ourselves to see our part in it. Many of us have held onto old resentments for years, stubbornly waiting for the other person to reach out to us. Instead of focusing on all the drama and betrayal of our resentments, maybe we needed to focus on the lesson at hand. We needed to face those people who still lived in our heads, and deal with all the negativity it produced in us. Perhaps we can ask God (or our sponsor) for clarity in seeing our part in it. Why did those people make us feel so uncomfortable? Why did they drive us crazy? Could we have been more tolerant? More patient? Maybe God placed this person we're resenting in our lives to teach us something important about ourselves, before we can move on with our lives. Maybe we should thank these people who triggered these strong emotions in us and who can push our buttons, sending us into a rage? Just maybe, these people are our real teachers! People will either be a blessing or a lesson to us. In life, some people will test us, teach us, use us and hopefully bring out the best in us. This is a spiritual program and way of life. We all want to experience peace, and the only thing that will bring us peace is our genuine, heartfelt forgiveness. Let the healing begin. Stop living as a victim. Stop buying into the excuses. Become accountable. Healing can only begin when we let go of the past. Put your energies to better use. It's the peace and serenity that keeps me coming back. Today, being at peace is more important than getting even. We are the ones who need to change.

• *What resentments are still interfering with your progress?*

• *What could be more valuable than peace of mind?*

"Nothing
is so bad . . . .

...that you have to sit down and *go crazy*"

– JOHN TELGEN

Many of us got use to living in a state of crisis. Repressing the pain, choosing not to deal with all our emotions, and medicating ourselves kept us sick for a very long time. Early recovery can also be a time of confusion and uncertainty, and the stress and strain we were under left many of us drained and exhausted. When I got to Alcoholics Anonymous I found myself on an emotional rollercoaster ride. My emotions were all over the place. I was bombarded with a wide range of emotions coming at me from all directions. I soon realized that they wouldn't go away on their own. This sudden flood of feelings that surfaced was overwhelming. I had a problem in articulating my feelings. I began to slowly process all the feelings I had worked so hard in the past to drown with alcohol. I couldn't allow them to remain trapped inside me. When they came knocking, I had to let them in. Denying them would only postpone the healing. I could no longer ignore, minimize, discount or suppress these emotions. Unresolved feelings will surface. They need my validation, attention and acceptance. Learning to live in sobriety involves acquiring new skills. AA prepares us for our reentry back into life by learning new and healthier ways to deal with all our feelings. We need to exercise patience as we work through this process. We begin to grasp things today that we couldn't have handled in the past. We've been lifted up and out of a "hopeless state of mind and body". A new energy is coming. We need to let these hard times be healing times. We haven't struggled in vain. It is also important to understand that time is not a threat, but a gift that has been given to us. We need to be content to grow a little each day. We can't expect our lives to change overnight. Let today unfold. It was gratifying to reclaim all those long, lost part of ourselves. Overtime we will become more able to live comfortably in the real world. When I'm having a bad day, I need to slow down and remember "easy does it". We need to approach life with an attitude of acceptance, patience and grace.

WITHOUT PATIENCE, LIFE WILL BE VERY FRUSTRATING!

• *What confusing emotions and feelings did you experience in early sobriety?*

"Shame can hold us back, hold us down and keep us staring at our feet."

–BEYOND CODEPENDENCY

The disease of alcoholism carries with it a stigma of shame, unworthiness and an overwhelming negative sense that who we are isn't okay. It got to the point that I couldn't even look people in the eye. I was painfully aware of the true depths to which alcohol took me. Shame is one of the most negative, all-consuming defects there is, and has fueled our addiction for years. I experienced a sickness so deep in my soul with unbearable remorse and agonizing guilt. I knew of the loneliness, the loss, the disappointments and the incomprehensible demoralization of this disease. We became objects of contempt to ourselves and we looked at our lives in more and more diminishing ways. Shame is a no-win situation and had fueled my illness for years. Shame kept me drunk. I was convinced that I brought nothing but pain and unhappiness to everyone I loved. I felt like a complete failure in every area of my life. One by one I got rid of everything good and decent in my life. I suffered in silence believing that I would never be enough. In the end, I couldn't separate the person from the disease. We were one in the same. This disease had become my identity. For most of us the struggle has been long, lonely and painful. I was just so tired of hurting. I was broken in spirit. I was one of the living dead. Coming to AA, I learned that I was suffering from an incurable, potentially fatal illness. I was not a bad person, only a sick one trying to get well. There is no room for shame or disgrace in sobriety. It was nothing short of a miracle that I found AA, where I learned how to talk about my pain. I learned that this pain is survivable. I was told that I needed to be able to look at my past with compassion for myself. No one wants to be forgotten, go unnoticed and feel unimportant. We all need to know that we count. We want to be appreciated, acknowledged and respected. Unconditional love is our birthright. Today I can share with others that there is a way out and that there is hope and healing! Younger alcoholics are coming into the program sooner than later, saving them years of damage and misery. In AA we reach out, connect, relate and share with singleness of purpose.

• *What effect has shame had in your life?*

• *How has it changed in sobriety?*

"The 1st duty of love ....

... is to listen"

–Paul Tillich

We need to learn how to become better listeners. I was an adequate listener. Part of our disease involved us not listening to what others were saying, which had kept us from hearing what we needed to hear to begin recovery. We needed to hear the truth. We wouldn't be in our present condition if we had simply listened to what our experiences (and our Higher Power) were trying to teach us! In the past, we had only heard what we wanted to hear, and had only seen what we wanted to see. Whether it was out of arrogance, or because of our controlling and fear-based egos, but we never liked being told what to think, do or believe. Finding AA changed all that. We needed to approach AA and the 12 Steps with a receptive and open mind. We'll never know where we will find the inspiration or the life-changing help and guidance we'll need to hear and process to recover. If I thought that that I had all the right answers, I'd stop searching and I'd stop listening. Nothing could be more dangerous for the alcoholic! Listening to others has helped us to get in touch with our own feelings. We needed to hear and accept the good as well as the bad in life; then and only then will we be truly able to deal with life as it really is. We needed to make ourselves available to receive new ideas and be able to apply them in our own lives. I no longer pretend to know what is best for me. I needed to learn to recognize my own limitations. In AA we become a part of something bigger than ourselves. I began to attend meetings. I listened, I identified and I bonded with others. I found that we shared the same worries and fears. I especially listened to others who had more time than me in the program and have walked the same path before me. I listened to how they dealt with this disease. I listened to their experience, strength and hope. I know today that I don't have all the answers, and that's okay. All I do know is that when I listen, I get better results.

The better I listen, the smoother my sobriety seems to go. It's amazing how someone I don't even know can say exactly what I needed to hear to help me with my problems. I listened and I heard my own story being told! I saw that I wasn't the only one who suffers. Some had it worse off. This fact helped me accept my disease. The things I heard gave me reason to hope. I wanted to keep coming back. I only wished I had listened sooner. I'm continually amazed about all the love, support, understanding and help I find just by listening! We are learning to listen a little better everyday. The better we listen, the better our recovery will go. When we don't listen we lose out on some wonderfully simple ways to improve our lives. Listening can be such a simple shortcut for positive growth and prevent us from learning some things the hard way! For the most part I have peace of mind today, and the war that raged in my head has died down.

•*WHAT WAS DIFFICULT FOR YOU TO HEAR IN EARLY RECOVERY?*

•*HAVE YOU BECOME A BETTER LISTENER?*

8

So many of us never developed the impor-tant life skills that we needed to take proper care of ourselves. We spent our lives judging, blaming and accusing everyone but ourselves when things went wrong. We usually saw ourselves as innocent victims of other's abuses and sought retribution for all the "justified" wrongs done to us. With Step Eight, we complete the housecleaning which is so necessary for putting the past behind us. Unresolved amends stood in the way of our recovery. Our alcoholism had neg-atively affected just about everyone we came in con-tact with. Our lies have spread out around us in ever widening circles of hurt. We finally have the oppor-tunity to get everything out in the open. We find the willingness to make things right. We begin to look at our part in any situation and take full responsibility for our actions. Step Eight asks us to consciously re-member and make a list of all persons we had harmed. We've all done things we weren't proud of. It's all about owning up to what we've done and become will-ing to free ourselves from all the guilt and shame our past actions have caused. What's important is that we deal with them and do whatever is necessary to right these wrongs. Forgiveness, signifying a healing change of heart, is the key to this Step. We need to remember that we did the best we could at the time. Step Eight is all about repairing and healing our relationships, restoring our self-esteem and bringing balance back into our lives. We come to realize that we are the ones who need to change! In Step Eight we concentrate on changing ourselves. A great relief awaits!

**66 When people talk,
listen completely-
Most people *never* listen."**

ERNEST HEMINGWAY

Have we become hard of hearing? Our addiction did something to the way we listened. We seemed to be suffering from "selective hearing". We heard only what we wanted to hear. Then there were others who had stopped listening altogether. Do you pretend to listen when you are really thinking about what you want to say next? Do you listen with an open mind, or are you defensive and closed-minded? Do you allow others to talk and share? Do you give others the time, attention and respect to express themselves and the chance to clarify their thoughts? The St. Francis Prayer points out that "it is more important to understand, rather than be understood." There have been so many times when we didn't listen with the intent to understand. We only partially listened with the intent to answer. Communication is a two-way process. We've missed out on so many lessons in life because we only wanted to get our point across. When we do all the talking, we leave no room for new thoughts and fresh ideas. In the past, our egos had kept us from learning the very things we needed to hear to be able to grow in sobriety. AA will work for anyone who will approach it with an open mind. We can learn so much about ourselves and others just by listening. We can begin to see beyond our differences and connect with others on a deeper level. As our hearts awaken, our sense of separation and isolation fades. It is one of the greatest gifts we can give each other - our undivided attention. All we have to offer anyone is ourselves, and this act of respectful listening often becomes the beginning of genuine sharing. The human connection is destroyed when we don't take the time to listen. All we are doing is creating further distance between us. We need to listen completely and be there totally for one another. By listening, we support and validate one another. We need to let others know that they count, and just maybe we'll learn something new. The need to change, grow and evolve is all part of being human. This can not happen in isolation. We are all here to help one another. We each play a very special role in each other's lives. By interrupting others, I finally realized how selfish and exhausting this behavior was. It takes a tremendous amount of energy to try to be in 2 heads at the same time! How did the other person react? Wait until it's your turn to speak. Give the attention back to him. Make him feel heard and listened to.

• *Can you remember a time when you "tuned out" someone because you wanted to do all the talking, or interrupted or finished other people's sentences or thoughts?*

❝ They love the best who love with compassion."

–E ᴌᴌᴇɴ Aɴɴᴇ Hɪʟʟ

Sometimes we need to be reminded that we are only human, and to be human is to be imperfect. It had been part of our survival routine to evaluate, judge and criticize imperfection in us and in others. Step Eight and Nine won't be effective without developing a personal empathy, a real caring attitude and a genuine concern about how others feel. Part of the healing process involves our striving to understand the other person. We are not the only ones who hurt. We begin to recognize that other people's problems, pain and frustrations, are as every bit as real as our own. Until we ourselves are hurt, we can never truly understand the pain of others. We know how it feels to live without hope. There is a saying, "in love's service, only the broken hearts will do." Out of our own suffering, we've been able to develop a deeper compassion. Those who make it to the rooms of AA are most in need of love, acceptance, nurturing, understanding and compassion. But as our illness progressed, we became totally unlovable! A newcomer needs to feel welcomed, not judged. They need to feel compassion and not contempt. They long to hear the words, "I'm so glad you are here", and "I'm totally here for you, I understand." We need to help in ways that support their dignity. Never be condescending; they need their pain and questions validated. It becomes a privilege to help others heal from the kind of pain and hurt we've all known so well. More than others, we can see their real and honest efforts and intentions beneath their mistakes and failures. When we were in pain, where would we have been without the compassion of others? Where is our sense of humanity? Unless we can comfort each other, hear one another's cries, feel one another's pain, celebrate each other's joys and cheer on each other's victories, we will be missing out on the best of what life has to offer. Everyday, one person's life touches another life in need of love. Many of us have only given lip service to our spiritual values. Many of us profess to be spiritual, but very few of us live it! A life of service is not a one time effort. Service is a lifelong process; it becomes a way of thinking about life. The words we say, the smiles we share, the hugs we give and the encouragement and hope we dispense all combine to create a statement about what we value most in life. That which does not come from the heart, will never be able to reach the heart. Each person enters our life for a reason, and no matter how brief the stay, brings enrichment and value to our lives. Love is the balm that heals our soul sickness. Let your heart be your eyes, and make yourself a source of love. Develop a forgiving and pardoning heart. Love is its own reward.

•*When was the last time you demonstrated your love through your actions?*

•*What can you do today to bring more love into your life?*

•*What do you do daily to remain humble?*

66 *Begin each day with a positive seed thought and hold it there*

–ROBERT SCHULLER

Negativity has a power all its own, and has been my own worst enemy. In early recovery I realized that I needed to stay away from those impossibility thinkers and others who were always looking for reasons why something couldn't be done, why it wouldn't work or why it was a bad idea. It was the type of climate that gave rise to skepticism, doubt, fear and pessimism. I couldn't stay mentally healthy if I continued to associate with negative people who would rather spend their time and energy whining about their lot in life instead of doing something to change it. The people most in need of love will ask for it in the most unloving ways. We needed to associate with positive people who can inspire and uplift us, who believe in us, and who support and encourage us, and avoid those people who'll pollute our minds, drain our energy and deflate our spirits. Negativity takes us out of harmony with the universe. We sought retribution for the wrongs done to us. But by insisting on our own measure of justice, we lost the ability to set and achieve positive goals. Negativity sabotages these goals and destroys our dreams. A negative mind will never give you a positive life. Our choices in recovery need to be positive ones. If something isn't working, we can accept it and choose not to dwell on the negative aspects. Whatever thoughts we give energy to, we empower. It's so easy to see what's wrong in our lives, but with daily practice, we can begin to see what's right in our world. We can't allow this negative energy to become a part of who we are. At the end of the day, I'm always amazed how many negative thoughts I've accumulated and all the lame reasons and excuses I came up with not to do the right thing. We begin to move our focus from our minds to our hearts. Take time to know your true self. Are you making a positive difference in your life? We finally have an opportunity to experience a sense of personal integrity. We've chosen to use our painful experiences to make a positive difference in the lives of other suffering alcoholics. I'm so grateful for all the loving and supportive friends and family in my life today. I am grateful for God's love and grace in giving me my sobriety. It's the love we carry within us that will make our lives in sobriety a success.

REMEMBER, A HEART FULL OF RESENTMENT, IS A HEART AT RISK. A GRATITUDE LIST IS A GOOD PLACE TO START!

- *What makes you grateful?*

- *Are you harboring any negative thoughts*

    that may be holding you back?

❝I can pardon everybody's mistakes except my own.❞

–Marcus Cato the elder

Recovery has everything to do with getting back a healthy sense of "self". We needed to deal with all the unearned guilt that we've heaped upon ourselves. Are we punishing ourselves for no reason? In my lifetime, nobody has ever abused me more than I have abused myself. I've denied and put down the only person I knew how to be. Over the years, this self-abuse grew out of years of self-rejection. I continually looked at myself in increasingly punishing ways. I looked at my mistakes as unforgiveable sins. It was self-inflicted misery. I was a victim of my own dysfunctional thinking. I thought my self-worth was beyond repair and that my life would never be any different. For years my drinking took me to places and situations I never wanted to go, and I was hurting more than I ever thought I could. I realize that I can't change the past with all the emotional fallout that has caused so much pain to myself and others, but I need to be able to heal from it. When I was told to make a list of all persons I had harmed, I should have put my name on the top. Punishing myself with self-sabotage thinking was never meant to be a part of my recovery work. It goes against everything the program of Alcoholics Anonymous stands for. I needed to forgive and let go of my "sick self" with compassion and self-acceptance. Our self-worth is the single most important ingredient that will influence all the choices we make daily. In recovery we learn about self-care, forgiveness and unconditional love. Making amends must be done in a spirit of self-love. I needed to throw away the Voodoo Doll! God, in His infinite grace and love, has given me a second chance, even when I had done nothing to deserve it. If God can forgive me, why can't I? We should never be defined by what we do or by what we have, but only by who we are inside and who we were meant to be all along. We have the power to make the choice not to suff er anymore. Pain is inevitable, but suff ering is optional! The time has come to leave our old self-defeating beliefs behind us. Loving thoughts will change our perception of everything. Our illness will always be a part of us, but for recovery to work we need to develop a nurturing and loving relationship with ourselves. Forgive yourself. How many real or imagined sins do we have to punish ourselves for before we can allow ourselves to enjoy life? Let yourself be human today. The only person you are destined to become is the person you decide to be. Do something today that your future self will thank you for. Make room for joy in your life. The purpose of recovery is for us to fi nd our true identity, inner peace and healing.

•*Have you been able to forgive yourself for being human?*

**" Pain is the touchstone
    of spiritual progress -
    It is a very human way
    of demanding change."**

-**12** AND **12**

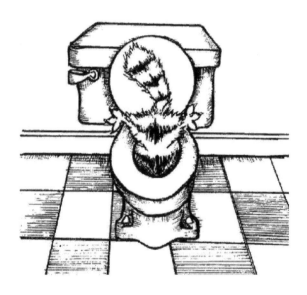

Many of us have found out the hard way that feelings of joy and freedom were not necessarily the reward of doing what we wanted to do. Very often pain and anguish were the end result, and at times the pain seemed unending. It's been said that pain is God's way of trying to get our attention. Pain can be a real warning sign that something is terribly wrong and we need to make some serious life-style changes. Little did I realize back then that the downward spiral I was about to experience would begin with the first drink! Little did I know of the devastation this disease would have in store for me! My pain had finally caught up with me, and as hard as I tried, even my drinking couldn't stop the pain. It only postponed it, and in the end once I drank, I didn't care. As alcoholics, we can tolerate a little pain for a very long time, but any undealt with pain will continue to fester below the surface until it erupts. Of myself, I had no power to help myself, and hitting rock bottom can be very painful, but also very purifying. Out of despair and humiliation, our priorities are made clear. I needed the trials and tribulations, the heartaches, the misery and the pain for me to find the clarity to surrender. Pain had to come before sobriety. I arrived to the rooms of AA spiritually bankrupt and broken. I wanted the pain to stop, and I didn't want to die. I could no longer sweep the source of my problems under the rug. AA gave a voice to my pain, and it was where I was encouraged to talk about it. In recovery we're shown how to deal with all the causes of our pain and are made aware of all the spiritual tools and resources available to us in the program. My wish for the newcomer is total desperation. I hope and pray they reach the point where they can no longer rationalize all their insane behaviors. I hope they run out of excuses and get very scared. If things hadn't gotten so bad, I may never have gotten the help I needed. Pain had pushed me to consider new choices. You must want sobriety more than anything else and be willing to go to any length to get it. Then there is nothing to stop you. It's been said that pain has been the price of admission into a new and sober life. Each sober day represents a milestone of what was once impossible for us to achieve. It was nothing short of a miracle that I found Alcoholics Anonymous. All the pain you are feeling now can't compare to the joy that's coming. Listen to your pain. It can be a great teacher. Your pain is survivable. I'm not telling you it's going to be easy, but it's going to be worth it.

• *What in your life was causing you the most pain?*

• *What do you do about it today?*

" Friends are the

... sunshine of life."

–JOHN HAY

Friends were missing in my life. There was a time when I thought alcohol was my best friend. It consoled me when I was upset. It helped me forget my worries. It helped fill the void of loneliness. I was prepared to follow it to the ends of the earth. Before coming to AA, my disease wanted all my attention. I had no time for family or friends -old or new. My life back then was one of increasing isolation, making human feedback impossible. I shared little of myself because I had nothing of myself left to offer to anyone. Overtime what I thought was my best friend turned into my worst nightmare. Drinking had become an obsession that dominated all my waking hours. For years I had sought comfort in the very thing that was determined to destroy me. In hindsight, I truly believe that God had placed new people in our lives for a reason. I'd like to think that friends are God's way of taking care of us. We no longer have to suffer alone in silence. We become the instrument through which God does His work. Out of our own suffering, we've developed a deeper compassion and have become acutely sensitive to the pain of others. It was this pain and suffering that becomes our connection to one another. Beautiful people don't just happen. The most beautiful people I know have known defeat, known suffering, known struggle, known loss, and have found their way out of the depths of insanity. These people have an appreciation, a sensitivity and an understanding of their lives that have filled them with a deep and honest empathy. Working Step Eight has helped us to reconnect with all the people we've shut out of our lives when we were drinking. In recovery we begin to need and want others in our lives again. It's the friendships that become important to us. No relationship carries a life-time guarantee, but if we are lucky enough to be blessed with a deep and lasting one, it becomes one of AA's most cherished gifts. Visualize God's healing light each day and send it to someone who is still hurting and in need of love. I no longer shut the world out. I can attend AA meetings anywhere in the world today, and I just know they will be filled with friends I just haven't met yet!

- *What things do you value in a friendship?*

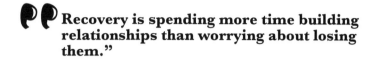 **Recovery is spending more time building relationships than worrying about losing them."**

–A<small>NONYMOUS</small>

Before entering recovery, we had trouble forming lasting, loving and successful relationships. We brought a lot of baggage with us when we came to AA: poor health, financial woes, fear of commitments, trust issues, fear of intimacy, fear of being alone, a compulsive need to people-please, immaturity, fear of asking for help, total self-absorption or total lack of self. We were neurotically needy and empty, with nothing to bring into a relationship, we couldn't even be a friend to ourselves. We used others and they became a superficial commodity. Many of us clung on to old relationships out of deep, emotional insecurities. Some stayed in abusive relationships. We were terrified of rejection. Our dependent personalities went from person to person looking for someone who would always be there for us. We entered into these relationships hoping to find the perfect soul-mate. The ability to form enduring and lasting friendships is what we strive for in sobriety. Wanting friends again in our lives is healthy and human. Step Eight has helped us to reconnect with all the people we've shut out of our lives in the past, and begins the process of healing our damaged relationships. Some of us are presently renewing old ones, and many of us are reaching out to new ones. It's the beginning of the end of our isolation. So much good can come out of healthy relationships. Relationships help us to be more human. In AA I've learned how to be a better mother, wife, daughter, sister, friend and co-worker. Friends love us enough to tell us the truth. They offer us strength and support, not pity. When scared or troubled, they become a sympathetic and patient listener. When adversity strikes, they are there, even if it's four in the morning. They bring out the best in us and inspire us to be the best we can be. Friends don't always tell us what we want to hear, but they tell us what we need to hear. They will love us unconditionally, faults and all. Don't take anyone for granted. Focus on the good in your life. Our greatest joys and our most cherished moments are the ones we've shared with others. Life is people. Life is relationships. Life is sharing.

• *Have your relationships been more real and honest in Sobriety?*

• *How are you improving your relationships today?*

9

NINE

> MADE DIRECT AMENDS TO SUCH
> PEOPLE WHEREVER POSSIBLE, EXCEPT
> WHEN TO DO SO WOULD INJURE
> THEM OR OTHERS

STEP NINE COMPLETES THE FORGIVENESS PROCESS THAT WE BEGAN IN STEP FOUR. WITHOUT FORGIVENESS, OUR LIVES WOULD BE AN ENDLESS CYCLE OF RESENTMENT AND RETALIATION. WE'VE BECOME ACCOUNTABLE AND READY TO ACCEPT THE CONSEQUENCES OF ALL OUR PAST ACTIONS, ATTITUDES, CHOICES AND DECISIONS THAT HAVE CAUSED OTHERS PAIN BY MAKING OUR AMENDS. STEP NINE HAS THE POWER TO RELIEVE US OF THE BURDEN OF GUILT THAT HAD WEIGHED SO HEAVILY ON US. FOR THE FIRST TIME IN A LONG WHILE, WE HAVE THE OPPORTUNITY TO EXPERIENCE A SENSE OF PERSONAL INTEGRITY. WE WERE EAGER TO SET THINGS RIGHT AND PUT THE PAST BEHIND US. WE ADMIT OUR WRONGS, FACE OUR FAULTS, ASK FOR FORGIVENESS AND ACCEPT RESPONSIBILITY FOR OUR PAST ACTIONS. THIS WILLINGNESS TO GROW IS THE ESSENCE OF ALL SPIRITUAL DEVELOPMENT. ACTIONS SPEAK LOUDER THAN WORDS. WE ARE FINALLY ABLE TO CLEAR AWAY THE WRECKAGE OF OUR PAST. TO BE TRULY FREE TO MOVE FORWARD WITH OUR LIVES, WE NEEDED TO MAKE PEACE WITH THE PAST. WITH STEP NINE, WE ARE GIVEN THE OPPORTUNITY TO CLOSE THE DOOR ON THE ALCOHOLIC THAT WE WERE. WE ALSO HAVE THE OPPORTUNITY TO CHOOSE THE KIND OF PERSON WE WOULD LIKE TO BECOME. WE JUST NEED TO TAKE THE ACTION.

"Alcoholism isn't a spectator sport, eventually the whole family gets to play."

–JOYCE REBETA–BURDITT

Alcoholism is a family disease, and one of the biggest misconceptions is that the alcoholic is not hurting anyone but himself. The truth is, the entire family suffers from the effects of this disease. There has been plenty of abuse, neglect, abandonment and betrayal to go around. The alcoholic family is anything but your "happily-ever-after" fairy tale kind of family. The family experiences the fallout from lost jobs, moving from state to state and changing of schools. Some families experience homelessness and are put on welfare. And alcohol doesn't discriminate; it's an equal opportunity disease. The people who love and care the most about us, usually suffer the most, as they painfully watch the alcoholic slowly kill her/himself. They become obsessed with the alcoholic and end up usually putting their lives on hold, neglecting their own needs and desires. Communication breaks down. The alcoholic says hateful things to family members, usually because that's the way he thinks about himself. Their entire lives become wrapped up in this disease, as they try to "fix" everything. They monitor the alcoholic's every move. They begin to lie, and they make excuses for the alcoholic. They invent cover-ups and they put great energy into looking good in public, never letting on what goes on behind closed doors. Family members have spent hours crying, screaming, threatening and pleading to the alcoholic to quit and get help. The family environment can go from loving and peaceful one minute, to out-of-control and threatening the next. With their hearts breaking, they cope the best they can. They've spent years trying to control the uncontrollable, and maintain order in an unpredictable and sometimes volatile home life. Without realizing it, the entire family comes to play a part in the dynamics of this disease; their survival techniques, like enabling, rescuing, etc. becomes a way of life. They managed to survive the chaos and pain, but did they? The effects of this disease can linger on, even in sobriety, unless they choose recovery for themselves. In order to overcome the devastating effects of this disease, and build and maintain a happy and healthy life, they needed to find new ways of dealing with their own obsession, anxiety, anger and denial.

• *How has your family been affected by your alcoholism? Your recovery?*

• *What are they doing to take better care of their own lives?*

**❝ The tragedy of a man's life is
what dies inside of him while
he lives."**

–THOREAU

U p to now, denial had made my life possible, and I practiced it without question for years. Denial ran deep within me and I had used it to protect myself from life's pain. But by the time I crawled through the doors of Alcoholics Anonymous, I was hurting, lonely and frightened. I believed I had no reason any more to live. Life was meaningless. I didn't value anything or anybody. God was absent in my life. I may have looked "together" on the outside, but I was dying on the inside. The lights were on, but nobody was home. My "perfect" little world was falling apart, and I could no longer pretend everything was "fine". In my progressive isolation, I was becoming more negative and cynical. Feelings of worthlessness, rejection and self-pity consumed me. I lived my life without joy, and I had used alcohol to avoid dealing with these unbearable feelings. I didn't like or even want to be around the person I'd become. I couldn't love or respect myself; I couldn't even be a friend to myself. I was running on empty. I was committing suicide by degrees; I was going nowhere and killing myself doing it. The shame and guilt were eating me alive. Day by day I was being drained of life's energy. Death had seemed to be an attractive alternative to my so-called "life". It seemed that most of the energy I had left went into trying to be invisible. I tried not to do anything that would call attention to myself. Thank God for meetings where I could share my despair and hopelessness. Instead of rejecting me, they loved me with open arms. They listened. They cared. Surrounded by loving and supportive friends, I was able to come face-to-face with my demons. This loving interchange sustains me to this day. There is great healing and restorative powers in connecting with other recovering people. I needed to confront this disease. I'm no longer a spectator, but am an active participant. I needed to find the courage to live, and I did in the rooms of AA. We are not only released from a compulsion to drink, but we are also guided towards a compulsion to live! We began to have more good days than bad days. The darkness in our lives will give way to light. I feel as though I've awakened from a deep, dark sleep. How sad it is that so many of us have escaped life. Life is waiting for our undivided attention. If you are experiencing any self-doubts that are holding you back, you are probably remembering the person you use to be. No one is born to lose or be a failure. Step Nine releases us from our heavy burden of guilt and shame, but it was only through positive action that we could achieve this relief. No matter how you feel, get up, get dressed, show up and never give up. What's the point of life if it's only about pain, anguish and worry? Don't make a bad day feel like you've had a bad life! Let's not cheat ourselves out of one more day of living. I don't want to look back at my life with any regrets. Each day offers us a chance to make a fresh start. What you make of your life is up to you.

• *What prompted you to finally want to take on Step Nine?*

" *What is defeat? Nothing but the first step to something better."*

–WENDELL PHILLIPS

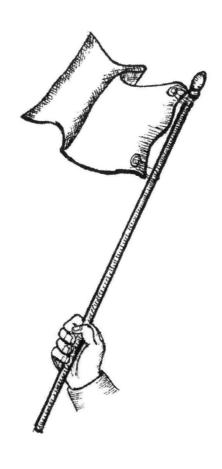

The program of Alcoholics Anonymous involves a series of progressive surrenders. In Step Three we surrendered by turning our lives over to a Higher Power. In Step Five we surrendered our deepest and darkest secrets, and in Step Seven we relinquished our shortcomings. In Steps Eight and Nine we surrender our anger, rage and resentments by making amends. Surrender gets the wheels in motion for our recovery. I use to let problems overwhelm me before I would surrender, and my repeated efforts to control a situation only ended up making my life more unmanageable. I've spent as much time resisting life, as I've spent dealing with it. If you are someone who always wants to do things your own way and has a strong and willful ego, then surrender may seem like defeat to you, but surrender only means defeat in battle. In recovery it signifies the transcendence of the ego and the release of it's control over us. Surrender is not something we can force or control by willpower; it is something we experience. This disease had finally beat us into a state of reasonableness. By hitting bottom, we quit playing God! It simply didn't work. Without any reservation whatsoever, we became ready to do anything to recover. We had no choice but to become more open-minded and more accepting of our human limitations. I had tried to make my life go my way, but it never did. I was driven to my own destruction by my stubborn need to be in charge. This disease grew stronger in my denial of it. I needed closure from this disease. Surrendering to a Higher Power is how we become empowered. In surrender lies great power. Strength arises from complete defeat. Our energies become channeled in ways that work for us and not against us. We need to pursue our recovery with as much zeal as we pursued alcohol. It's the process that enables us to move forward in sobriety. We were not brought into this world just to be defeated. If we want to live an emotionally happy and healthy life, we have to know how to handle the pain and hurt when it comes. Up to now, God was my last resort. Today I know that He stands ready to help. We can't move forward by resisting; we can only change and grow through acceptance. I needed to put my energy where it could do some good. By letting go of my self-will and stepping out of the way, I've opened up the door for help. I pray I never take back my misguided power. We may experience some short-term discomfort, but we'll reap long-term benefits – a beautiful sober life!

• *How are your surrenders progressing?*

• *Have you been tempted to take back control?*

"Making amends isn't just saying I'm sorry. It means responding differently from our new understanding."

–AS WE UNDERSTOOD

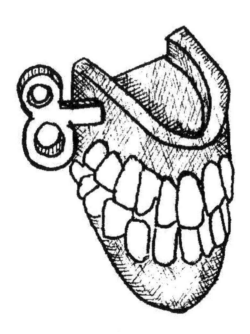

We had to do more than not drink to prove that we had changed. Not drinking was just the beginning. We had to do more. We're not "cured" just because we had stopped drinking. If we really wanted sobriety, and if we really wanted to live a sober life, we had to make some major changes. For us to continue to blame others offers no hope for any improvement or change. If I wanted others to believe that I've really changed, I needed to back up what I said with action. Talk is cheap. Understanding without accountability is just as wrong as accountability without understanding. Recovery is so much more than lip service and mindless chatter. The outcome remains in God's hands, but the effort must be ours. When change is called for, it's a change we must initiate. It's amazing how quickly we can regain our credibility when we walk the walk. Taking no responsibility for changing what was in our power to change all along is over. It's our behaviors that tell others who we are becoming. Making amends is the logical continuation of the recovery work we began in Step One. Amends must be made to those we had harmed, injured, insulted, cheated, abandoned, neglected or otherwise wronged. We make amends for things we have done, and for things we have failed to do. Making amends is not the same as apologizing. Making amends requires action to make up for our past wrongs, like keeping broken promises, volunteering, returning stolen goods, telling the truth and giving time and support to a person we've neglected. Making amends and righting our wrongs is a wonderful unburdening and cleansing process. It also brings into play all the qualities we're aspiring to in sobriety, like honesty, humility and responsibility. People around us will begin to react differently to us; we can see it in their faces, their voices and in their reactions. The world hasn't changed, but what has changed is how we live our lives today. Ironically, the changes I most dreaded making have been the ones that have set me free, and have had the most positive influence on my life. Open your heart, nurture patience, keep promises, bury regret, discard hate, transcend self-doubt, don't dwell on the past and build a better tomorrow. With each step we take, we'll feel a little better, a little safer, a little prouder, a little lighter, and a little freer. The Steps have given us the chance to start fresh, offering us the support, encouragement and guidance we so desperately needed to start us in sobriety. We've developed a plan of action. I no longer dread change. I look at it as a time of celebration. Changes are gifts that signify successful and positive growth.

• *Why is saying you're sorry just not enough?*

❝ If you are distressed by anything external, the pain is not due to the thing itself, but to your own perception of it.❞

–MARCUS AURELIUS

There are so many things we have chosen to believe about ourselves that just aren't true. I've had to review all the things that I've been telling myself all these years. Alcoholism is also a disease of perception. We've carried around a faulty belief system that has become stronger and more impenetrable over time, even when we were exposed to new and positive beliefs about ourselves! We found that our old beliefs still controlled our lives. As a result, we never really acquired the ability to make an accurate self-appraisal of ourselves. It was part of our disease to compare and evaluate. There was something within us that found the need to judge and criticize all our actions, thoughts, feelings and appearance over the years. We tended to interpret and label everything and everybody as either good or bad. Over time, we came to believe in a distorted image of ourselves. We used words against ourselves like "I'm too fat", 'I'm losing my hair", "I'm getting old", and "I'll never be good enough". When we doubt ourselves and our worthiness, we sabotage our efforts to recover. By the time we reached AA, we had become the primary recipient of all this negative pollution and fallout from this disease. Sobriety is a journey of personal transformation. We're all here to transcend our perceived limitations. In sobriety we come to realize that we all possess the ability to turn any situation in our lives into either an insurmountable problem or a valuable lesson. It all depends on our own self-image which impacts all the choices and all the decisions we make in every area of our lives. When we continually relive our mistakes, real or imagined, over and over in our minds, we end up believing that we are only partially deserving of God's grace and of life's many gifts. When we were born, we had no concept of "good or bad", or "right or wrong". Our troubles were to be found in our evaluations. Why do so many people undervalue what they are and overvalue what they're not? We don't perceive things as they really are. What we see is colored by our expectations, assumptions, faulty beliefs and our fears. What upsets us most in life is our perceived ideas in our heads of how life is suppose to be. What others do or say is a projection of their reality, not ours. Likewise, your opinions are no one's truth but your own. This disease has taken away my freedom, my dignity and my self-respect. Recovery is giving it all back. Being who we are is the greatest thing that will ever happen to us in our lifetime! Be an authentic original – it's always worth more than a copy. Begin today to tell yourself how wonderful you are. Do it often. Don't ever let anyone dull your sparkle!

• *Were you aware of all the distorted images you had about yourself?*

• *What has become clearer to you in recovery?*

❝ Sometimes its more important to discover what one can not do than what one can do.”

–LIN YATANG

So many times I've heard the saying, "we're not human beings in search of a spiritual experience; we're spiritual beings in search of a human experience." A recurring question that we want answered is, "who am I?" and "what is my purpose in life?" By the time I reached AA, I was broken in spirit. I had no idea who I was. I couldn't relate to the world around me. Because of my addiction, I felt hopelessly flawed and unworthy of love. I had squandered all my God-given talents and had lost sight of all my dreams. I was filled with a sense of missed purpose. What were my gifts to share with the world? The real tragedy is that so many of us punished ourselves relentlessly for our imperfections. I've spent most of my life devaluing my talents, achievements, hopes and dreams. I've come to look at recovery and working the 12 Steps as a pilgrimage of sorts, where I find my way back to my real self. The Steps have breathed new life into me. I persevere daily to uncover my imperfect human side of myself. The truth is we all have infinite potential within us. The greatest waste by far is the waste of this undiscovered potential. I'm through apologizing and doubting myself. I have nothing to prove! I've reclaimed my own spiritual identity. I needed to find my own voice and be able to stand in my own light. There was a time when I thought my life was over before it began. I felt I didn't have anything special to share with the world. We've been given a second chance to live a worthwhile life. I will never allow this disease to define me ever again. Being human and imperfect are not character defects! God has a beautiful plan for all our lives and wants to inspire everyone to be all that they can be. The future belongs to those who believe in the beauty of their dreams. You are here to do wonderful things. Let your light shine. Find something that inspires you. Share it with others. Enjoy the process of your own life. Our dreams that once had appeared impossible to attain are now back within our reach again. Life is what we make it. Don't be pushed around by your problems. Be led by your dreams. Fall asleep with a dream and wake up with a purpose. Remember, you can do anything, but not everything!

• *What things do you do imperfectly today?*

Intuition is a spiritual faculty and does not explain, but simply points the way."

–FLORENCE SHINN

W e're confronted with so many decisions to be made in our day-to-day living, yet for most of our lives we've felt so ill-equipped to make the right choices. Growing up we were taught not to trust our instincts, so they basically went undervalued and unappreciated. We were taught to be logical and use our powers of reason to think rather than feel our way through life. We believed we couldn't possibly know something without thinking it through. We were told to apply rational thought and sound judgment. If an experience defied a logical explanation, we dismissed it as inferior to the human ability to reason. As a result, we've been navigating our way through life using only logic as a compass and guide, often getting lost in our own limited thinking. But in AA, we came to see that logic and reason alone weren't enough, and were no substitute for intuition. Sometimes knowledge and facts don't hold all the answers to life. Trusting our instincts is an essential step in our recovery and spiritual growth. It was suggested that we find spiritual solutions to what was essentially a spiritual disease. This was difficult in the beginning because we had become so spiritually disconnected from ourselves. We came into the program without a strong sense of identity and low self-worth. The biggest trust issue we had was simply learning to trust ourselves. In the past, we were always worrying about whether we were making the right decision. Gradually, we become aware of the spiritual resources that were available to us. We needed to have faith and believe that our intuition is guiding us to a greater good. Over time, it became more and more natural to turn within for answers. We became more God-reliant. What good is divine knowledge if we don't tune in to hear it? I have spent too much time working against my better instincts! Today, when I have a decision to make, I need to search my heart, not my head for answers and higher guidance. We've dwelled long enough in the confines of our own minds. Our hearts know things that our mind can't begin to explain. By learning to trust my intuition, I regain an essential part of myself. What a disservice we do to ourselves when we do not listen to these internal messages. I need to practice "checking in" regularly. I need to pay more attention to what I feel inside. Educating the mind without educating the heart, is no education at all. If it feels right, it usually is. In the end, intuition is a very reliable source of superior wisdom and spiritual guidance. I no longer attempt to explain with reason and logic alone why things happen. Following this spiritual path has changed my life. Today, I know that I can live and grow through difficult times. I won't let the noise of other's opinions drown out my own inner voice. I look to the day ahead with wonder and trust. Liberate your own inner awesomeness! I don't know what the future holds, all I can do is make the most of each day.

• *In what areas of your life are you trusting your intuition more than you did before recovery?*

10

STEP TEN

CONTINUED TO TAKE PERSONAL
INVENTORY AND WHEN WE WERE
WRONG PROMPTLY ADMITTED IT

STEP TEN HAS BEEN CALLED THE MAINTENANCE STEP PROVIDING US WITH A S FORMULA FOR CONTINUED HEALING. THIS STEP BECOMES OUR DAILY RITUAL AND NIGHTLY REVIEW, GIVING US THE OPPORTUNITY TO DO OUR BEST EVERYDAY. IT ALLOWS OUR LIVES TO REMAIN IN GOOD WORKING CONDITION, SAFEGUARDING OUR GAINS AND KEEPING US AWAY FROM UNNECESSARY BURDENS. STEP TEN IS A PROGRAM OF DAILY ACCEPTANCE AND REMINDS US THAT THIS PROGRAM CAN ONLY BE SUCCESSFULLY TREATED AND ARRESTED ONE DAY AT A TIME. BY PROMPTLY ADMITTING WHEN WE ARE WRONG, THIS STEP ALSO CHALLENGES US TO BE HONEST ON A DAILY BASIS. IN THE PAST, WE DIDN'T DEAL WELL WITH LIFE. WE HAD BECOME EXPERTS AT MANIPULATING THE TRUTH. WE WERE QUICK TO EXCUSE, BLAME OR JUSTIFY ALL OUR MISTAKES. STEP TEN KEEPS US ON TRACK. I'VE HEARD STEP TEN BEING REFERRED TO AS THE "TAKING CARE OF BUSINESS STEP". IT BECOMES OUR GUIDE IN OUR DAILY SPIRITUAL JOURNEY OF RENEWAL AND GROWTH, RESTORING BALANCE AND HARMONY TO OUR LIVES. IT ALSO REMINDS US TO ALWAYS LOOK AT OUR PART IN ANY SITUATION AND TO BE WILLING TO SEE ANOTHER POINT OF VIEW. THE NEXT TIME WE DO SOMETHING THAT BOTHERS US, WE CAN PROMPTLY ADMIT IT. IT'S A SIMPLE FORMULA FOR TAKING LOVING CARE OF OURSELVES. THE TENTH STEP IS ALL ABOUT SELF-EMPOWERMENT. WE NEED TO LET THE PROCESS HAPPEN.

" *You miss 100% of the shots you never take."*

–WAYNE GRETSKY

There are no born losers. If I fail, I know I'm in good company. Consider: Babe Ruth had 1,330 strike outs, Einstein didn't talk until he was four, Beethoven's teacher said he was hopeless, Pasteur's teacher told him he was mediocre in chemistry and Michael Jordan was cut from his high school basketball team! This is the life we are given. Our job is to make the most of it. If we are not giving our best to life, then we are not living up to our full potential. Giving our best is not something we do at random when the spirit moves us, it's something we do everyday. We need to stop obsessing about our failures and setbacks and begin to think about the opportunities we missed out on when we didn't try. In hindsight, looking back over my own life, I gave up on just about everything I had ever tried in life. It took Alcoholics Anonymous to make me reexamine what success is. Isn't winning really a matter of rising each time we fall? Winners are not people who never fail, but people who never quit. In meetings, we're told to "keep coming back", especially after we've relapsed! Each time we slip, we need to get right back up on our feet and try again! Success or failure is not so much determined by all the external resources that we've claimed we lacked, but rather by our own belief, or lack of, in ourselves. Obstacles to success exist more in our minds than in our abilities. People fail in life, not because they lack ability, intelligence or opportunity, they fail because they don't give their lives all they've got. Most people succeed, not because they are destined to, but because they are determined to succeed. The only person stopping you is you! We learn by making lots of mistakes. In the beginning, your failures are more valuable than your successes! It's very human to make mistakes. Nothing can be learned without failing somewhere along the way. How are we suppose to learn and grow in life if we never fail? We should welcome obstacles. They are the real stimulus and motivation to success. We need to transcend all these perceived limitations in order to make extraordinary things happen in our lives. In recovery we get off the bench and get into the game of life. The present moment is the field on which the game of life is played. It can't happen anywhere else. If my mind is on the past or future I'm in a powerless state. Today I'm not a quitter. In the end, we'll only regret the chances we didn't take. Don't quit before the miracle. Remember it's the rebounds in life that make the difference! It takes courage to try something and fail, than to never attempt to do anything and succeed.

• *What have you given up on in life that you wish you hadn't?*

" A relationship can't be healthier than the people in it."

–MARY KAY W.

We are all looking for greater fulfillment in our lives. We not only used alcohol to relieve our pain and medicate our miserable reality, we also used our relationships to help us feel alive and whole. Overwhelming fears and insecurities have kept us in co-dependant relationships for years. We've spent most of our lives fighting a poor self-image. We've depended on others to complete us and give us a sense of identity. We went from person to person hoping to find someone to make us feel a whole lot better about ourselves. I relied on others to validate my feelings, my thoughts, my needs and my likes and dislikes. It was no wonder that so many of our relationships became smothering, unhealthy and one-sided! In recovery we learn about who we really are, independent of our parents, our spouses, our children, or our friends. Before we can bring anything positive and healthy to a relationship, we must first learn to love, honor and respect ourselves. How can I share myself with others if I can't acknowledge what I'm thinking or feeling? How can I share myself with others when I need you to define me? My first relationship must be with myself. Co-dependency is a spiritual issue stemming from a lack of spiritual wholeness. In recovery we begin the task of deciding what we like to do, how we want to spend our time, what books we want to read, what foods we like to eat, etc. We discover our value as an independent, whole person. Our identity must begin on the inside. The only person who can love me the way I want to be loved is me. Today I approve of myself, I honor my choices, I enjoy my own company, I am a friend to myself, I trust myself, I accept that I'm a work-in-progress, I cherish every part of me – flaws and all, I am my own person, I am happy, joyous and free, and I deserve the best life has to offer. Today, I can share myself with you and you can share yourself with me, without either of us trying to change the other. We can support one another and still give each other room to grow. Many of us entered into a relationship hoping to find ourselves, but we lost ourselves instead. We became less happy, less capable, less motivated. In sobriety, relationships are based on choice, not neediness. When two people come together, they become greater than the sum of their parts.

• *What qualities do you bring into a relationship today?*

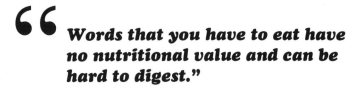

" *Words that you have to eat have no nutritional value and can be hard to digest.*"

–ANONYMOUS

The way we relate to others depends upon how well we communicate. It's not only what we say that's important, it's how we say it. Words are powerful tools that we use to think, create, express ourselves and communicate with others. Part of owning our power in recovery is learning how to communicate clearly and directly. Our words are a gift from God, and through them we are able to manifest everything. The thoughts that shape our lives, what we dream, what we hope for and all we envision and feel are manifested in the words we use. Words can be used positively to give support, hope and encouragement to a person to keep trying. Everyday, we have the opportunity to make someone feel a little better about themselves. When you plant a seed of love and kindness, it is you that blossoms. How you make others feel, says a lot about you. Be the reason someone smiles today. Our words have the power to create beauty, but they also have the power to destroy. Words can do more harm than good. They can even be used as weapons to judge, evaluate, measure, compare and condemn. They can be used in a state of fear to deceive, control, sabotage and manipulate. Words can become toxic when they are used to express anger, hate and contempt. Words can reinforce our fears or can discourage someone who's struggling. Words are used to prey on another's vulnerability with idle threats and unwanted advice. We need to be clear about our motives. Is there a hidden agenda behind our words? Do we say what we mean, and mean what we say? Do we say "yes" when we mean "no", leading to a resentment or worse? Do we make promises we can't keep? Do we back up our words with appropriate actions? Do we think twice or count to 10 before we speak in anger? We've abused and misused words for years. Disagreements can be a constructive experience or a brutal attack. Words can help clear the air or they can undermine our progress. In recovery, we're learning more diplomatic, appropriate and kinder ways to express our thoughts, ideas and feelings. We take into consideration other people's feelings. When we speak from our hearts, others will be more receptive to hear what we have to say. When we speak with kindness and compassion, we become the kind of person we're striving to become. In AA meetings all over the world, the message of Alcoholics Anonymous is spread using words to recount the gut-wrenching tragedies as well as the amazing miracle stories of recovery. We use words in the best sense to share our experience, strength and hope to others still suffering.

• *What qualities do you bring into a relationship today?*

• *How have you used and manipulated words in the past to get what you wanted, that may have harmed others?*

❝❝ You don't get to choose how you're going to die, or when. You can only decide how you are going to live.❞

–Joan Baez

L ife is what we make it. Our purpose defines us. Our destiny is not beyond our control. We have within us everything we need to manifest and live the life we desire. The dreams that once appeared to be impossible to attain are back within our reach. It only requires our willingness to begin and follow through with the work required to live a sober life. Sobriety requires daily upkeep and it is so important to prioritize our day-to-day activities and to continue to diligently take our inventory. There will be times when we may think that we are cured and no longer need meetings or even the program of Alcoholics Anonymous. If we find ourselves slowly reverting back to old patterns of thinking, feeling and behaving, we really need to get to a meeting! We need to be able to correct these trouble signs when they show themselves. We've been given the tools to identify and handle these warning signs before they handle us. We must never get too complacent, or we will find ourselves headed for a slip or worse. If sobriety doesn't seem as important as it once was, if we find ourselves keeping secrets, if we begin to work the other person's inventory, if we are isolating more than usual, if we reject help or are too afraid to ask for it, if we stop calling our sponsor, or if old thoughts of controlled drinking surface...wake up! We need a reality check! I'm an alcoholic, and there's no amount of hiding, denying, begging, praying, ignoring or over-thinking this disease that will change this unchangeable fact! My priorities have changed in sobriety. What's important to me today is who I am as a person. What matters today is how I live my life. My success in the program is due, in large part, to my becoming a part of something bigger than myself. My new life is all about making good choices, and living authentically with integrity. Everyone is born with a purpose, but until we find out what that purpose is, we may feel like a puzzle with some of the pieces missing. We may have a sense that we're here to do something here on earth, but what? For the time being, carrying the message of AA to the alcoholic who still suffers is a wonderful purpose. We've been given a second chance to live our lives with a purpose. There were others in the fellowship who came before us and laid the foundation for our recovery and healing. That was their gift to us. The way to return that gift is to pass it on to the next person who will be filling our shoes. Never give up on your vision. The hardest part is getting started. Help others learn what you've learned. Be the example that they can follow. Live your values and follow your heart.

• *What are the priorities in your life today?*

• *Have you found your purpose?*

• *If you knew that you could not fail, would you do it?*

❝ Gladly accept the gifts of the present hour.”

–HORACE

During the time of my active addiction, one day was like any other – long, lonely, painful, guilt ridden and shame filled. It was a time when I couldn't see past the lies, the problems, the negativity, and the incomprehensible demoralization we know only too well. The disappointments of daily living kept me from appreciating all that was good and decent in my life. I had looked at my life as a burden rather than a gift. In sobriety, we've been given the gift of life and we need to cherish each and every one of these days as a priceless gift, whether we have 30 years or one day of sobriety. All any of us have is today, and we need to make full use of it by giving the next 24 hours our undivided attention. Today is before us. The next 24 hours will be unlike all others, and will never be repeated. One day at a time, by setting reasonable and manageable goals for the next 24 hours, we can surprisingly accomplish anything we set our minds to do. Our confidence may waver from time to time, but being open to the present is our only chance for growth. We have spent too many days dwelling on the past and the future, and we ended up missing out on today's opportunities and joys. We began to realize that there is more to life than problems. Take a moment to think about what it means to be alive. We need to put our gratitude into action everyday. I'm grateful for the privilege of being able to fully experience another sober day and be able to share it with people I love. I'm grateful to be able to hug my children and watch them grow into extraordinary human beings. I'm grateful to be able to see, hear, smell, touch and feel life that is all around me. I'm grateful for being able to enjoy the colors of a rainbow or the setting sun. And, I'm grateful to be able to see a newcomer light up when he/she "gets" the program; it is a gentle and important reminder where I came from. It's so sad that too many alcoholics don't stay around long enough in the program to receive these most precious gifts. Lastly, I'm grateful for a thankful heart. No matter how crazy my day has been, I must never forget to be grateful for what I have, for my growth and for my healing. Sobriety is truly a gift that keeps on giving. Take the time to experience the miracles that are all around you. God has given this day to us as a gift, but what we do with it is our gift to Him. Why not, just for today, be thankful for everything? When was the last time you watched the setting sun, felt the warmth of the sun on your face, walked barefoot on the beach or felt the gentle breeze blowing through your hair? (How many days have we wasted drinking, hung over or blacked out?)

• *What are some of the gifts that you've received in sobriety?*

"Optimism is essential to achievement and is also the foundation of courage and of true progress."

–Nicholas Murray Butler

W e've come such a long way on our journey. Big changes are happening to us. We can see progress. Most of our excess baggage is gone! We have a new life and a new path to follow. To keep on track, however, we need to keep looking at ourselves. Taking our inventory will be a lifelong process of self-examination and spiritual growth which we began in Step Four. This inventory can be looked at as a balance sheet for the day. First, we need to recognize and promptly admit our mistakes. But we also need to acknowledge our progress and focus on all the things we are doing right! We begin to take notice of all the wonderful aspects of ourselves that we may not have given ourselves credit for in the past. We need to focus on our character assets and accentuate the positive. It would be a sad, sad day when we haven't done something right! Even on our worst days, surely we can find one thing that we did right. Finding the positive in ourselves may be new behavior for many of us. Undoubtedly, we will make some sort of mistake everyday of our lives, but we shouldn't limit our inventory by focusing only on the negative. Optimism fills the rooms of AA. We begin to find things to feel hopeful about. I keep coming back because the program helps me feel so good about myself. I try to make each day better than the last, as I grow daily in my faith and confidence in my abilities. In the end, we become the primary beneficiary of this thorough and honest inventory. Our lives in sobriety come down to integrity, being authentic, trusting God, being honest, cleaning house and helping others. Doing inventory work is a wonderful promise I make to myself everyday. There was a time when I thought all things were possible. I believe it can be that way again. For years we didn't live, we merely existed. We've been blessed with a new sober life; we've been reborn. We're learning about new ways to enjoy life. Did I demonstrate courage today? Did I keep commitments today? Did I practice gratitude and acceptance today? Did I set healthy boundaries? Did I venture outside my comfort zone? Did I take responsibility for my actions? Did I practice forgiveness" Did I face my fears? Did I express my needs to others? Did I accept criticism? Did I express my feelings appropriately? Did I find time to meditate and pray? Celebrate the miracle of this transformation in you. Step Ten gives us the opportunity to do our best everyday. I try to make each day better than the last.

• *How has Step Ten made a difference in your life?*

❝ ***Never grow a wishbone where your***

backbone ought to be.❞

-CLEMENTINE PAPPLEFORD

My sobriety to date does not guarantee a ticket to future sobriety. Sobriety is hard work. There are no shortcuts or free rides. There is no easier, softer way. We know all too well the futility of trying to overcome our addiction by willpower alone. The program tells us that we have to work for change, and not just wish for it. For years I tried to wish away my disease, but this disease will not go away on its own. Up until now, many of us had been unwilling to do the work needed for recovery to proceed. In sobriety, we confront our disease. The stakes are high. All that we've gained in recovery could be lost if we let up on our program. I have to make a conscious decision everyday to recover. Recovery is not about easy. I needed to find the courage and the strength to change my life. Once and for all, I needed to take responsibility for myself and my life. We must rise to the occasion, roll up our sleeves and be ready. We're up against a formidable opponent that is not going to give up without a fight! We need to understand that our character defects will continue to reappear from time to time. AA is not a resting place. When tough times come, and they will, we'll need a positive program of action. There are so many ways we can sabotage our recovery. Gone are the excuses we use to buy into. Excuses kept us from taking an honest look at ourselves. We must never make excuses for our drinking, good or bad. Excuse making became habit forming and we mastered it to perfection. Every excuse we make is a choice on our part to fail. We've been given life-saving tools; we need to use them. As our recovery progresses, we begin to replace our self-doubts with new confidence in ourselves. Doing Step Ten has become part of my daily routine. Today, I am an alcoholic, and I will be one tomorrow, and the day after that, and the day after that. AA is not something we leave behind. It becomes a way of life. I've always had problems facing reality, but because of AA, there is no problem in life that I can't get through today. Don't hide behind all your excuses. Stand tall!

• *Is there some situation in your life that you've been hoping would magically get better if you wished long enough?*

• *Which of your defects of character have reappeared most often?*

• *What are you doing to keep it in check?*

11

STEP ELEVEN

> **Sought through prayer and meditation to improve our conscious contact with God as we understand him, praying only for knowledge of his will for us and the power to carry that out**

By the time we reach Step 11, we can definitely attest to the fact that some power greater than ourselves is working in our lives. Daily communion with God is very important to our recovery; it's as crucial as breathing in and breathing out. The nearer we draw to our higher power through prayer and meditation, the closer we will be to our source of serenity, strength, guidance and healing. It's important that this channel be open and free of all the confusion and static of our daily lives. These quiet times restore us to sanity. We so often felt serenity slipping away from us, and we used to struggle to know His will for us. We needed God's loving discipline to keep our willful natures in line. Just as our bodies need discipline, exercise and nourishment, our spiritual selves need to be replenished. This daily routine of prayer and meditation will keep us in fit spiritual condition. Our goal is to be physically relaxed, emotionally calm, mentally focused and spiritually aware. By practicing prayer and meditation, we are given a daily reprieve from our disease, but it is contingent upon our spiritual condition. It's important that we take whatever actions we can to improve our conscious contact with the God of our understanding. We need to continue to seek His will for us, so we will be more able to face whatever the day ahead brings us. Prayer and meditation strengthens and renews our source of well-being everyday.

The passing moment is

it is only common sense to

all we can be sure of . . . .

extract it's utmost value."

–W. Somerset Maugham

We create our own stress everyday. I've always had a tendency to overdo things and rush headlong into all my daily activities. I got impatient with anything that slowed me down. I was forever trying to make things happen by setting impossible deadlines for myself. I use to worry that if I didn't push myself all the time nothing would get done. Why do we try to do so much in such a hurry that we fail to give ourselves totally to each moment? This urgency has put such a distance between our Higher Power and ourselves, taking us farther away from our serenity. There must be more to life than increasing its speed. Is getting more things done in less time going to make a positive difference in my life, or will it just increase the pace at which I react to people, places and things that seem to be controlling my life? Is there something I needed to see in a deeper way? We live in a society that thrives on urgency. We live on fast foods, crash diets and minute rice. We depend on overnight deliveries, pagers and the internet. The world is at our fingertips. There aren't enough hours in a day to get everything done. We can't eliminate all the stress in our lives, but we can simplify our lives by prioritizing. AA is a simple program. Fewer experiences are of less value than fast sobriety. Even the Promises do not materialize overnight! Like all good things, recovery takes time and it involves a long-term healing process. I know that if I put my sobriety first, everything else will fall into place. We need to be content to grow a little each and every day. I'm learning that for today, time is going at just the right pace, any faster, and I wouldn't have enough time to learn all the lessons that life is trying to teach me. I was told, "easy does it". Everything is right on schedule. Today when things don't happen according to my schedule, I can accept it.

• *What activities did you rush around doing?*

• *How important were they in the scheme of things?*

" The light of **God** surrounds me, The love of **God** enfolds me, The power of **God** protects me, The presence of **God** watches over me, Wherever I am, **God** is."

–Prayer Card

God is everywhere. I know He is real. I talk to Him. I feel His love for me. I see His spirit manifested in loving relationships and friendships. I see Him in the beauty of nature that is all around me. I feel His presence in the music I listen to, in the poetry I read and in the paintings I admire. I see Him in the twinkle of someone's eye, in an understanding nod, and in an affirming wink or a warm embrace. I hear Him in a child's laughter and in a grieving person's tears. I see Him in the faces of everyone I meet. I believe, without a doubt, that He is the living part of AA. I see Him in hundreds of miracles that are happening all around me everyday. I know He's real, He's my closest friend. It's important for me to take the time to know Him, to hear Him, to understand Him, to honor Him and to draw near to Him. Someone once said that God is either everything and is everywhere, or He is nothing. My conscious contact with Him is my constant source of comfort, guidance, serenity, courage and wisdom. He helps me turn my suspicions into trust, my doubts into faith and my anger and resentments into forgiveness. He guides me through my most challenging decisions and my most overwhelming fears. I search out his guidance in everything I do. God has given me new dreams and goals. He's helped me to tear down my walls of isolation and is helping me to build bridges instead. Today, I will not allow negativity to stop the flow of God's love. I will let my heart speak, and I will pray for the willingness to accept God's will for me. Each time we connect with our Higher Power, we are heard, touched and changed for the better. No prayer ever goes unanswered. In my darkest hour, I remember crying out to God to help me. To this day, I'm convinced that He carried me into the rooms of Alcoholics Anonymous. Like so many others, I came to Alcoholics Anonymous not believing in anything. Today, the love I've found here is like the love of a caring parent, comforting their lost and hurting child.

• *Have you asked for God's help today?*

Enjoy the little things, for one day you may look back and realize that they were the big things."

-ROBERT BRAULT

In recovery, we need unconditional love more than ever. Our addiction had cut us off from others. By going to meetings and sharing, we've begun the healing process of opening ourselves up to loving and being loved back to health. Pain has had its purpose in our lives. It was one way we had been connected to one another. In recovery we are no longer alone, and when we let others know that they're not alone, we can heal. Today, I will cherish another's presence by reaching out to them. Each day provides us with opportunities to ease the pain of another. Today I will offer love and kindness where it is needed. I will allow my heart to rule. When we begin to trust in the program, in a Higher Power, and in the goodness of life, we'll respond more positively to life. For so many years I didn't feel grateful about anything. I had been giving all my power away to how bad I felt, to my lack of finances and to how unfulfilling my life has been. The day-to-day pressures and disappointments have kept many of us from appreciating the small things in life, let alone the big things. Even if we don't think we have anything special to offer anyone, we need to share the little that we do have. Often a single act of kindness can set in motion more acts to follow. Each act of kindness rewards us with many positive feelings. It's the little things that bring enormous satisfaction and peace of mind. Ask yourself what is really important in life. Was I kind? Was I forgiving? There are so many ways to make a difference. Reach out with compassion. Give your undivided attention to someone. Share hope. Offer a kind word to a stranger. Make coffee at a meeting. Everyday that we commit to our recovery we will find a little more peace and a little more love. The quality of our lives is determined by the gifts we choose to give. Become a silent angel today. Everyday we have a chance to make someone feel a little better. And when we make someone else feel special, we become special too. It's one of the beautiful aspects of the program because it embodies the beauty of God's plan for all of us. We are connected to one another. Every loving gesture soothes our souls, and even helps to contribute to a healthier, saner, and more loving world. Positive actions, if only an understanding smile, makes for spiritual wellness. I will put unconditional love into action today. When I reach out, I know I'll always receive more than I give. We need to see love, feel love and return love. Only then are we truly doing God's will on earth. Take responsibility for how you touch and connect with others. Live by your actions. Remember, what we do in life will touch the lives of so many others. Raising another's spirits can make their day. It can even save a life.

•*Where are you putting your energies today?*

•*What kind gestures have you offered to someone else today?*

Through the dark and stormy night, Faith beholds a feeble light, Up the blackness streaking; Knowing God's own time is best, In a patient hope I rest, For the full day-breaking!"

–JOHN GREENLEAF WHITTIER

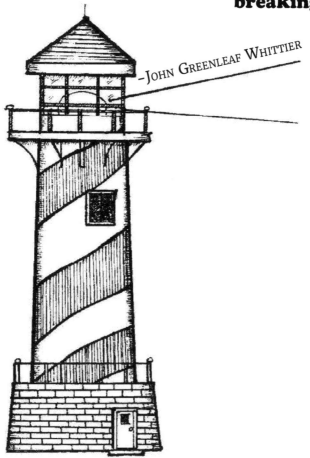

Sometimes we can't see more than a few feet in front of us on our journey through life. I got tired of stumbling over obstacles and groping my way around in the dark. It got to the point that my life had very little light, and navigating through life, using only my logic as a compass, left me feeling lost and alone. All my past struggles and fears were a testament to my attempts to do things all alone. There is no need to act out of fear or force solutions any more. A better way beckons. I've discovered that God was never far away. When all human resources have failed us, there is one who is at our disposal 24-7. Everyday and in every moment there is an unlimited resource of divine guidance, insight and strength available to us that will guide us through the most challenging decisions and the most overwhelming fears. He guided me when my life was at its darkest. God, or our Higher Power, is here, all around us, like a beacon on a lighthouse, always there to help and guide us through the storms of life to safety. There will be moments of darkness and uncertainty when we will not be able to see our way clear to the truth. Too often, I have gotten lost in my own limited vision and thinking, but today my faith has become a beacon in times of confusion and darkness. Divine love guides me and is helping me stay on course. Today I make it my top priority to keep my mind and heart open to receive all of God's messages. Recovery has given me the chance to move beyond the limits of the past. My vision may still be limited at times, and I may still veer off course for a while, but I know God's love will guide me back to my true path, every step of the way. When God guides me, I am given strength and I am shown the way. Today, I remind myself that I am sober by the grace of God, and that any success I may achieve is far more His success than mine. The path ahead may be easy or hard, but today I walk in the light of God's love, peace and joy. Through God's grace, I've been given the opportunity to live another way. Finding faith in a Higher Power has changed my life. I've found a peace and a happiness I had forgotten existed. My life is on course today.

• *How has your Higher Power guided you in troubled times?*

" **I** *will be attentive to all the signs from God today. Whatever answer I seek is finding its way to me.*"

–Each Day A New Beginning

In everyday life, the need for life-changing decisions arise that many of us have felt too ill-equipped to make. There will be moments of confusion and uncertainty when we can't see our way clear to the truth. Complexity is a fact of modern life, but reason alone doesn't have all the answers to life. Things happen that I do not understand or comprehend. I often got lost in my own limited thinking; I've spent too much time working against my better instincts. I know I don't have all the answers, but today, when I don't know what to do next, God does. I believe that God speaks to each of us throughout the day, and if we open ourselves up to these messages that are all around us, we will find the answers we seek. Part of our disease stemmed from the fact that we rarely listened to what others were saying. In this fast-paced and confusing world, we need to be willing to set aside time for meditation and our sincere and humble request for higher guidance and clarity. We need to empty and quiet our minds of all the mental chatter and external stimuli, so we are better able to receive the solutions that are on their way to us. Clarity is coming, and more will be revealed when the time is right. It is in these quiet times that we are more able to leave all the insanity of life behind us. These quiet times brings me an inner peace that I haven't felt in a long time. But, how much can God give to us if we're not open to receive? Meditation allows us to feel a oneness with our Higher Power. God is not separate from us. He is the creative force behind everything we do and see. He created us, and we are special for no other reason than that we are. Our "conscious contact" is strengthened each time we tune into this spirit. Let go of your feelings of separateness; we are all part of the universal consciousness. Prayer and meditation will always provide us with the answers we seek. There is a right solution and outcome for every diffi culty. Answers may come to us from anywhere when we least expect it. Meditation restores us to sanity, by allowing us to experience the loving presence of God. And when the answers we seek aren't quick in coming, I can trust that God will provide us with new ways of seeing. The answers are as close as our quiet moments. We need to listen. We don't have the time not to meditate. Find a way to set aside a few minutes of your busy day for refl ection, it will reap tremendous benefi ts. We'll be less reactive, less ir-ritable, and we will gain clarity and perspective. Balance will be restored in our lives. Like most things in life, meditation takes diligent practice.

Does meditation come easily for you?

how do you achieve a peaceful state?

What has been your experience?

Perhaps the fastest growing spiritual movement in the world today is the 12 Step Program."

–KEITH MILLER

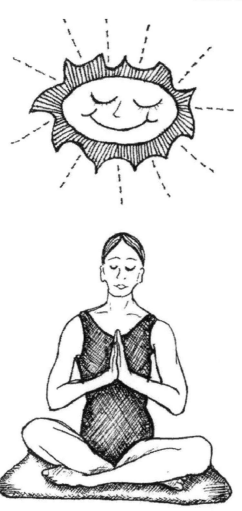

Only two things are asked of us when we decide to join Alcoholics Anonymous. The first is that the only requirement is the desire to stop drinking. The second point is that we must be willing to grow along spiritual lines. I consider myself to be one of the most fortunate people in the world today, because I've tapped into an extraordinary, life-changing phenomenon called Alcoholics Anonymous. I get everything I need today from Alcoholics Anonymous. I've not only found a second family, but I've found a place where I can be myself and be accepted for who I am. I've never been a joiner, but I remember crawling into the rooms of AA a sick and broken human being, and I've never regretted this decision. Being a member of AA doesn't mean my life will become problem free, but it offers me hope, because it is all about making changes. We come together to laugh, to cry, to rejoice, to console, to offer encouragement, and we come away changed people! Together, we can keep the Promises coming true. By being part of this fellowship, we'll be insuring that the suffering alcoholic who makes it to AA 50 years from now will have the same life-saving opportunities that we have all had. The spiritual way of life is its own reward. I have a restored relationship with a God of my understanding, with myself, as well as with others in and out of the program. While many of the world's religions judge, divide, separate, exclude and control their members, the spiritual program of AA is inclusive, non-judgmental and offers unconditional love to one and all. We face life together. As my alcoholism progressed, my circle of friends grew smaller. Today, I share this journey in sobriety with real friends by working the 12 Steps of Recovery. Our hearts reach out to one another as we share our experience, strength and hope. Because of AA, I've been shown that there is a way out of my misery. As alcoholics, we had stepped outside the circle of life. But as our hands join in the closing prayer, each of us becomes part of a circle of hope that is greater than any of its individual differences. By praying for others we become aware of the unity of all life. We are not isolated beings struggling alone. Our happiness is linked to the happiness of all. By belonging to something larger than ourselves, we've come to feel the security and protection of a larger reality. For this I am eternally grateful. Each time I come away from a meeting, I can feel the healing love it offers that I can't get anywhere else. Someone once said that there are only 2 things in life that are certain – death and taxes. Because of AA, there is one more thing. When anyone in the program is hurting, I know that the hand of AA will ALWAYS be there. The fellowship always makes me feel so much better, so loved and so at peace with the world.

• *How do meetings make you feel?*

"LOOK WITHIN THE SECRET IS INSIDE YOU."

-HUI-NENG

On my spiritual journey from ego to spirit in recovery, I've discovered within myself something quite extraordinary and very precious. There is a place inside each of us where a wonderful doorway exists. It's a place where I can detach from my busy schedule and go to, and it's been waiting for my return. It was here that I found God. There is an enormous power inside of us which does wonderful and loving things for us. We have the power to manifest our heart's desire, and attract all that we could ever want or need. We need only embrace and believe in it. I had nearly lost sight of the fact that I am a spiritual being, and that serenity, peace, love and joy are God's promise to us. His love flows through me when I have the willingness to open up my heart. My self-esteem had been so diminished that it had been difficult to believe that God could ever exist in me. In the past, I had not made room for God in my plans. But today when doubt and confusion wash over me, I have an "unsuspected inner resource" that I can tap into on a daily basis, telling me I'm enough. Many of us have been on a quest for deeper fulfillment. That quest is over. The secret to life has always been inside us. Finding happiness is no longer an act of gratifying the ego. Maintaining our spiritual condition is crucial in sobriety. Some of us have tried to externalize God, and others have tried to intellectualize Him. We did everything but feel him working in our lives. I've found a wonderful place within. I not only comprehend the word serenity, I actually feel the sunlight of His spirit. It's a peace I haven't felt in a long time. I've opened up my heart to a power that fills me with love and acceptance everyday. It's a power that loves me just as I am, on the good days as well as the bad. Prayer is a kind of calling home everyday. My prayers are simple. I express my gratitude for all I've been given and I ask for the strength and wisdom to do His will. My morning prayer sets the tone for the rest of the day, and is probably the most important appointment of my day. Today God is a constant in my life, and all he asks of us is to take the time to draw near to him. I can not be where God is not! As long as I have faith, my path is clear. Don't squeeze God into your life or give Him your left over minutes. Don't use Him as a last resort, and never wait to pray only when you are in trouble. I'm so grateful that God didn't give up on me, even when I was ready to give up on myself. If light and love are in your heart, you'll find your way home. You're the one He's been waiting for!

• *Have you developed a routine for prayer?*

• *How has the quality of your life improved since*

you've come to rely more on your Higher Power to guide you?

12

TWELVE

HAVING HAD
A SPIRITUAL AWAKENING
AS THE RESULT OF THESE
STEPS WE TRIED TO CARRY
THIS MESSAGE TO ALCO-
HOLICS, AND TO PRACTICE
THESE PRINCIPLES IN
ALL OUR AFFAIRS

Each of us has a unique journey ahead of us. We began our journey alone and frightened, clinging to the little bit of control we had over our lives. We began working the steps and shared the program with others. AA is a life-changing program where we learn the difference between staying sober and living sober. We felt reborn, filled with hope and freed of all the fears that have prevented us from living the life we were meant to live. We've undergone an incredible transformation, a radical change in our perception in the way we see ourselves and others. By working all the Steps, we can finally connect the dots. We came to see how our drinking was but a symptom of a far graver issue — our inability to live life on life's terms. Many of us may never have found this amazing, sober way of living, had it not been for all those who took the time to "see" the human being beneath our alcoholic exterior. AA is not something we leave behind when we get better. It becomes a way of life that we'll never outgrow. But sobriety is only the bare beginning. We want to share AA's message of hope with others who still suffer, and we are grateful for any opportunity to pass on this gift to others. We simply can't help others without uplifting ourselves. It's a privilege to share this remarkable journey with others in the program. The spiritual "rule" is that you can't keep it unless you give it away. To watch the eyes and heart of another awaken to God's presence in his/her life makes our lives so worth living. We become living proof that miracles happen.

Thank God for Alcoholics Anonymous!

" God gave you a gift of 86,400 seconds today. Have you used one to say thank-you?"

–WILLIAM A. WARD

So often the disappointments of daily living kept me from appreciating all that's good in my life. I've spent too many years focusing on negative and destructive messages. As a result, I became cynical, skeptical and desensitized. I had been giving power to all the wrong messages, like how bad I felt, how awful I looked, how rotten my day had been, or how depressing my life was. Gratitude became the antidote to all the negativity I've been feeding myself over the years. In recovery I'm learning to build upon the good in every moment by counting my blessings. It's a conscious choice I make daily. Sadly, too many alcoholics don't stay long enough in the program and never receive these precious gifts. My life today is a gift that holds many more gifts within it. This attitude of gratitude is magical because it turns everything we have into enough. It's all about empowering the good and positive in my life. A thankful heart is a gift of the program. I have real friends today and that is a wonderful gift. We are gifts to each other. Hope and faith are also gifts that we receive in sobriety. Being able to give and receive love is a gift. The opportunity to grow is a gift. Our peace of mind and our good health are gifts. The freedom to live in the moment and a life of endless possibilities are such precious gifts of the program. The opportunity to be of service to others is another gift. Even painful and difficult times, as well as all our mistakes and failures are treasured gifts, because they offer us clarity, humility, strength, empathy and wisdom. All of life is a gift if we are receptive and open to it. More and more I found myself smiling for no particular reason. Concepts of God crept into my vocabulary. The good feelings I was experiencing began to carry over into every area of my life. The gratitude I found in AA swept over me like a tidal wave. I will never take anything for granted ever again. There are no ordinary moments in AA. Each and every moment is an irreplaceable miracle. How does someone go from a hopeless state of mind and body to a full and thankful heart? Join us in Alcoholics Anonymous!

• *What gifts have you received in sobriety?*

" To know the road ahead, ask those coming back."

-CHINESE PROVERB

W e've tried, in many half-hearted and often quite innovative ways, to recover from the disease of alcoholism on our own. To make a long story short, it didn't work! Up to now, we had only wanted to hear what we wanted to hear, and do what we wanted to do. When we first entered recovery, I don't think any of us realized how sick we were or that we were fighting for our lives! We came to Alcoholics Anonymous with many unanswered questions. Early recovery especially is new and strange, and we didn't yet know our way around the program, the meetings or the Steps. It was suggested that we find a sponsor and to stick with the winners. Sponsors offer help, comfort, support and encouragement to the newcomer by sharing their experience, strength and hope with us. A good sponsor, however, is not a pushover. A smart sponsor offers tough love. Sugarcoated platitudes are of no help to the newcomer. It was important that we find someone we could share our most humiliating and not-so-perfect life experiences with, without being judged.

WE NEEDED TO FIND A SPONSOR WHO GOES TO A LOT OF MEETINGS, HAS WORKED THE STEPS, SOMEONE WHO PUTS SOBRIETY FIRST AND MAKES AA A WAY OF LIFE 24/7.

A good sponsor will be able to alert the newcomer about the twists and turns of the road ahead; where it will be bumpy, where the potholes are, where there might be dangers and when and where to slow down. Many of us would not be here today if it weren't for the love, help, special friendship, dedication and selfless service of a sponsor. Newcomers are the life blood of AA. To make a difference in someone's life, to watch them grow in the program and improve the quality of their lives is a priceless reward and becomes the highpoint in a sponsor's life. Someday it will be our turn to guide others along the same path. We will be able to tell them that the rewards they will receive will far outweigh their present pain. We almost lost our lives to this disease. We are not just devoted followers, but we become a living demonstration of what is so right in this program. There is so much still to do to carry the AA message of hope and healing. No one is without a contribution to make. We are sober today because someone, somewhere reached out a hand to someone who was suffering. There will always be someone with less time than you. Reach out to them and let them know that you understand what they are going through. When we extend our hearts and hands, miracles happen. Keep on trudging that road of happy destiny! Sobriety – what a wonderful place to be today! You don't have to be brilliant or rich or smart to be a sponsor, you just have to possess a caring heart.

• *What qualities do you look for in a sponsor?*

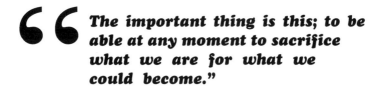

The important thing is this; to be able at any moment to sacrifice what we are for what we could become."

–CHARLES DU BOS

We've spent most of our lives hiding deep inside ourselves, fighting a poor self-image. We had become spiritually disconnected from ourselves. God gave each of us wings when we were born. The greatest tragedy is that so many of us never got to fly; we remained earthbound. This all changed in recovery. There is a beautiful you waiting to emerge. Wonderful changes are taking place in our lives today. We are becoming transformed and freed from our past and from the bondage of self. There is a beautiful YOU waiting to come out. In recovery we are discovering a new spirit that is guiding us, loving us, teaching us, encouraging us and nudging us in the direction we need to go. The really difficult and confusing times of recovery are nearly behind us, and the pain of self-understanding has made us stronger. With each Step forward or backward, we've learned to accept where we are in life with gratitude for everything that has brought us to where we are today. A new energy is coming. We've awakened from the nightmare of our disease. We are emerging into radiant, successful, intelligent and caring human beings. With each new lesson we get to experience personal growth with love and compassion for ourselves. This power has shown me how goodness, mercy, forgiveness, compassion, hope and faith, and strength and courage are wonderful attributes to aspire to. This Higher Power has been my teacher in times of confusion, my comforter in times of sadness, and the healer of my pain. Recovery is like a metamorphosis where we become aware of "becoming". Just as sure as a caterpillar will emerge from its cocoon into a beautiful butterfly, our true selves are also emerging. We've struggled to believe in ourselves, but our struggles have not been in vain. We've come through great suffering with our disease, shedding our cocoon of shame, guilt, old destructive behaviors and self-hate to become who we were always meant to be.

YOU'VE GROWN INTO AN IMPERFECT, INEVITABLY FLAWED AND BEAUTIFUL HUMAN BEING TODAY. IT'S UP TO YOU TO DISCOVER WHAT IT IS THAT MAKES YOU THE WONDERFUL PERSON YOU ARE. IF YOU QUIT, YOU'LL NEVER KNOW WHAT GREAT THINGS YOU MIGHT HAVE ACCOMPLISHED! SOBRIETY IS AN INCREDIBLE LIFE-CHANGING, LIFE-AFFIRMING JOURNEY.

• *What dormant qualities are beginning to emerge in your recovery?*

Some people regard discipline as a chore. For me, it is a kind of order that sets me free to fly."

–JULIE ANDREWS

Do you value peace of mind? Self-sufficiency? Independence? Daily attention to discipline is the surest road to obtaining these freedoms, and while freedom is our birthright, it ultimately must be earned. Sobriety is freedom, but with it comes great responsibility. I use to see discipline and freedom as opposites. I saw discipline as limiting my choices, and forcing me to do things I really didn't feel like doing (dieting, exercising and going to meetings, etc.). Sobriety requires hard work and serious commitment, but my old, impatient and disorganized nature longed for instant results. Wanting to have it all at once has been a recurring problem, as has our desire for easy solutions and half-measures. I didn't want to work to reach my goals, I just wanted to "be there"! For too long we passively watched and waited for our lives to change. Unfortunately, we won't wake up one morning and be non-alcoholic! Life is waiting for our undivided attention. Our whole approach to life had to change. Sobriety doesn't just happen. AA is not a resting place. There is work to be done. In recovery we work hard at taking better care of ourselves. Recovery is far too important to leave to chance. We needed to stop looking for easy solutions. All that we have gained in recovery could be lost forever if we let up on working our program. We've worked hard to get to where we are today. We came to realize that the program will work, if we work it. We work the steps until they become part of us. We needed to become active participants in our own lives. We can not expect our Higher Power to do for us what we can and must do for ourselves. We must never drift back into complacency, apathy or indifference. Continuous sobriety requires continuous effort. Achieving what we really want in life requires discipline on our part. It means staying with something, no matter what! Discipline isn't easy or fun, but it is the best friend we'll have in early recovery. AA is a spiritual program of action. Sobriety is for doers. For without the action, there can be no results and no rewards. Discipline forms the foundation upon which we can build a strong and secure sober life.

• *What kind of discipline was most helpful for you in early recovery?*

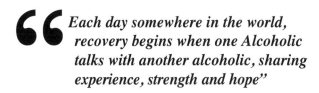

Each day somewhere in the world, recovery begins when one Alcoholic talks with another alcoholic, sharing experience, strength and hope"

–ALCOHOLICS ANONYMOUS

AA is a fellowship that puts great faith in collective healing. AA is a shared experience. Our paths have crossed for a reason. We come together and become united against a common enemy – alcohol. We not only survive together, we also thrive together. By helping guide someone else, our sobriety is reinforced. It's how we make sure the program will still be around tomorrow for those who'll enter the program after we are gone. The good we do each day will live on. We were like a sponge soaking up a new and positive way of living, giving us the strength to carry on. Many of us came to AA doubting that there was any reason to hope for a better life. If we had continued to struggle alone, in all probability we would have died. We are the survivors of the same shipwreck – addiction. But if we all work together, chances are we will get back safely to shore. We're living proof that miracles do happen. A new world has opened up to us. We are perhaps the luckiest people in the world today to have found a place where we truly belong and where we can be ourselves and are accepted for who we are. Feelings of uselessness and self-pity went away, and we could begin to see how our experience could help others, no matter how far down the scale we have gone. By sharing our experience, strength and hope we are able to carry this amazing, transformational message of Alcoholics Anonymous. We don't have to earn a seat; it is freely given to those who have a desire to stop drinking. We've inherited an awesome responsibility in sharing what has worked for us to turn our lives around. If our willingness does not remain a priority, we stand in danger of losing it all. Today I will give AA my enthusiasm, my devotion, my time, my attention, my support and myself. I'm not telling you it's going to be easy, but it is going to be worth it! Ironically, by losing ourselves in helping others, we ultimately find our true selves.

• *How has sharing with another alcoholic helped you in recovery?*

The first time I ever heard the Twelve Steps read at a meeting, I became very still....I knew deep within me that I was home."

—AS WE UNDERSTOOD

Our strong wills had to be redirected. But I could not have done this without the help of the 12 Steps of Alcoholics Anonymous. Millions of people all over the world are recovering from addiction using the same 12 Steps to change the course of their lives. For years I've resisted doing anything others suggested I do. It wasn't until all the painful consequences of my drinking became so unbearable, that I became willing to do to work necessary to begin my recovery. The Steps help us find solutions to problems that have robbed us from a rich, full life. We access their healing power by working them on a daily basis. There are no complicated meanings or messages, no hidden agendas, no shortcuts, no magic formulas, no potions or pills to make our addiction go away. The Steps become our "How to Guide" enabling us to make peace with the past, to live in the present, and to eliminate our old, destructive character defects. The Steps teach us about forgiveness for ourselves and others. They show us how to take responsibility for our own lives and actions, and they challenge us to be honest everyday. The Steps also help to process all the discomfort, awkwardness and pain we experienced in early recovery. They help us to become aware of our human limitations and let go of all the things in life that were never ours to carry in the first place. The Steps are also brilliantly designed to clear away the baggage of our egos. The Steps even help us to rediscover and deepen our spirituality.

They allow us to walk through any problems life throws our way. We will never out grow or be done with them. We live the Steps. Each Step becomes an invitation to discover who we are

THE STEPS HAVE BEEN REFERRED TO AS THE "GATEWAY TO HEAVEN HERE ON EARTH"

and who we are capable of becoming. By working them, we are given a life-long remission from this disease, one day at a time. The Steps have made it possible for me to live a life of honesty, humility, selflessness and service. We no longer have to stay stuck in our misery and our dysfunctional attempts at living ever again. The Steps become the tools we use to reclaim our lives. They've given me back my dignity, my self-respect and my purpose and reason for living. Trust them to rebuild your life too. The Steps will help illuminate your path in sobriety. How I wish the entire world would live by them!

• *How has working the Steps improved your life?*

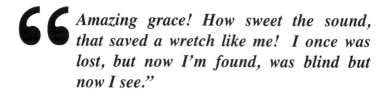

Amazing grace! How sweet the sound, that saved a wretch like me! I once was lost, but now I'm found, was blind but now I see."

-JOHN NEWTON

Whenever I see others who are still suffering from the disastrous effects of alcoholism, I think, "there but for the grace of God go I." Here were others who desperately wanted to awaken from the nightmare of their addictions. They were living their lives in utter hopelessness. This disease had drained their lives of all joy and meaning. Most of them were clueless on how to live a sober life and deal with their anger, shame, frustration and self-loathing, and turn it into compassion for themselves and others. Why is it that out of this seemingly hopeless situation, some are given the strength to rise above their addiction, and others are not? It remains a mystery to me. My own pain and suffering have taught me to be more loving and compassionate to others. If it weren't for the grace of God, I could have easily been in their shoes! Working the program on a daily basis has allowed me to heal and grow. I've become more tolerant, less impatient, less critical and less resentful. Today, rather than complaining, finding fault, criticizing, feeling short-changed and bitter and wallowing in self-pity, I work conscientiously to keep gratitude as my chosen attitude in every moment. Life itself is an unearned gift, and practicing gratitude will help me to more fully appreciate what has been given to me. I take nothing for granted today. AA has helped me replace my victim mentality with an attitude of gratitude. I ceased being a victim and became empowered by God's grace instead. My life began to change from the inside out. The term "spiritual awakening" is no longer an abstract concept.

IT IS A SHIFT IN CONSCIOUSNESS AND A PROCESS WE UNDERGO THAT WILL TRANSFORM EVERYTHING WE DO AND SAY !

It's an act of grace in which we're powerless to make it happen or prepare ourselves for it. I've come to know a new freedom, a new peace and a new happiness. Life's beauty and wonder were there all along, but it was impossible to see when our souls were filled with such darkness. The rainbow will appear after the storm has passed. Darkness will give way to light. AA has helped me to open my eyes and heart to let God's grace, love and light shine through. I thank God not only for the good parts, but for every single thing that has brought me to this awakening. I simply had to reach out and take the hand of AA that was there all along. Don't turn your back on Him. God could and would if He were sought.

• *How has God's grace blessed your life?*

"WHEN THINGS GO WRONG, DON'T GO WITH THEM."

–ANONYMOUS

There have been days when I thought the good times would never come again and that nothing positive could ever come out of my alcoholism. How I longed to be able to take a vacation from my misery. Avoiding anything unpleasant became a way of life for me. We indulged in the dream that tomorrow we would somehow be richer and happier. For so long we thought a different job or home would make all the difference in the world, bringing us the happiness, acceptance and love we longed to find. It became an unending quest. But alas, all our unhappiness and problems always seemed to come right along with us! Our search for serenity often took us farther from it! I've learned that I can be dysfunctional anywhere! We finally realized that running away from our problems is a race we can never win. It finally occurred to me that everything I'm running away from is in my head! We need to accept that in life we're going to have problems, set backs, rejections and disappointment. They are an inevitable part of life. We needed to understand that we had also played a crucial role in creating our own misery! By working through all the 12 Steps, we can now gain perspective on our life in sobriety. When the hard times come, and they will come, doing a geographic is no longer an option for us. We had to stop chasing after the "high". We are where we are today because of the fear-based choices we made in the past. Life in sobriety is a day-to-day journey of self-discovery, sometimes painful, but more often one of joyful discoveries and unexpected treasures. We need to be open to what is coming next. We shouldn't be in such a hurry to move on. Changes are something to be embraced, not feared or run from. We're here on earth to experience life, not escape it. We've come a long way in sobriety. The gifts of the program are evident everywhere in our lives.

"FOLLOWING THE 12 STEPS HAS ENABLED ME TO GROW UP.
SURRENDER TO WHAT IS, LET GO OF WHAT WAS AND HAVE
FAITH IN WHAT WILL BE."

DON'T POSTPONE HAPPINESS.

- *How are you showing up for life today?*

- *Did you do a geographic move?*

- *Did it make your life better?*

P.S.....

THE SECRET TO HAVING IT ALL, IS KNOWING...

...THAT YOU ALREADY DO!!

LIFE WILL TAKE ON NEW MEANING. TO WATCH
PEOPLE RECOVER, TO SEE THEM HELP OTHERS,
TO WATCH LONELINESS VANISH, TO SEE A FEL-
LOWSHIP GROW UP AROUND YOU, TO HAVE A
HOST OF FRIENDS — THIS IS AN EXPERIENCE YOU
MUST NOT MISS!

A Note from the Author

Sobriety is a precious gift that I have received from working the 12 Steps of Alcoholics Anonymous on a daily basis. My love for and my belief in these Steps have prompted me to write a workbook entitled, "The 12 Step-12 Week Plan". As a grateful recipient of all wisdom, joy and freedom that I've received from working the Steps, I've been given the opportunity to carry the message of AA to others who still suffer from this cunning, baffling and powerful disease. For the first time I feel that I have something valuable to contribute and give back to the program. The Steps are something that I will "live" for the rest of my life and are the guiding force in my life today. It took hard work to get to where I am in my sobriety, and in hindsight, I am so grateful that I kept coming back. It has taken me a long time to understand, forgive and feel good about myself again. Today, my disease no longer defines who I am. My on-going sobriety has returned me to myself, my humanity and to my God given potential. For the first time in years, I've found the desire to draw again, and I feel that there is no greater purpose in my life than for me to utilize my art as a tool to help others heal. All that I've been given in the program grows and grows the more it is shared. Recovery is not an end, but is a bright new beginning of endless possibilities!

Made in the USA
San Bernardino, CA
22 January 2016